Understanding *The* Holy Spirit

Dr. Brenda
Rambo

Understanding the Holy Spirit by Dr. Brenda Rambo
Published by Creation House
A Strang Company
600 Rinehart Road
Lake Mary, Florida 32746
www.strangbookgroup.com

Design Director: Bill Johnson
Cover design by Justin Evans

Library of Congress Control Number: 2010925932
International Standard Book Number: 978-1-61638-173-8

First Edition

10 11 12 13 14 — 9 8 7 6 5 4 3 2 1
Printed in the United States of America

DEDICATION

Dedicated to my grandchildren, Jay, Carson, Drew, Bella, and Sean, with the prayer that they will carry the power of the Holy Spirit to the ends of the earth.

CONTENTS

ACKNOWLEDGMENTS

I WOULD LIKE TO take this opportunity to thank Jamie Chavez for her editorial expertise in taking a manuscript that was written from my heart to the body of Christ and doing such a wonderful job.

I would like to thank the many seasoned intercessors who have taught me much and prayed many long hours with me. Their passion for Jesus made me hunger for more of Him.

I would like to say thank you to my husband, Mike, as he supported and watched me struggle and fight to overcome numerous obstacles to bring forth this book.

To my family and friends who love me and support me with their love and concern, I am grateful.

And Debbie Barry, you are the one who cheers me onward and upward to the high call of God on my life. I will forever be grateful for our friendship.

INTRODUCTION

He will baptize you with the Holy Spirit and with fire.
—Matthew 3:11

From the beginning of time, the Holy Spirit was with God; He was the creative power source that brought forth God's universe. One of the enigmas of the nature of God is that He is one being, yet three persons: the Father, the Son (Jesus), and the Holy Spirit. Admittedly, this is a difficult concept to grasp, and perhaps it's best left as a divine mystery, but for the sake of a simple explanation, consider this: I have a sister, which makes me a sister. I also have a husband; thus I am a wife. I have children, too; this means I am a mother. I am a sister, a wife, and a mother; I'm the same person, but I have three roles. And whether I am acting as a mother, wife, or sibling, my fundamental character doesn't change.

Thus it is with the triune God. And while the God of the Old Testament and Jesus, the Son of the New, seem to get much of the attention, the Holy Spirit runs as a current through it all. This book discusses the most overlooked person of the Godhead and His role throughout human history.

The Holy Spirit is the power source that brought forth the miracles of the Old Testament—moving through the prophets, kings, and ordinary men and women—establishing and performing His Word and unfolding His story (history). In the New Testament, He was the power behind the immaculate conception of Jesus through the Virgin Mary and the source of Jesus' power while on Earth.

The Holy Spirit is the One who draws and woos us to Jesus during our conversion and salvation process. When we are baptized, we are infused with the Holy Spirit; He gives us gifts to advance His kingdom. With the baptism of the Holy Spirit, a gateway to power, supernatural experience, and divine revelation is available to us.

As we mature in Christian faith and learn to hear the voice of the Spirit, we will start to experience the gifts of the Spirit—such as wisdom, knowledge, prophecy, or discernment—and know how to use them for the good of ourselves and others. As we grow in the fruit of the Spirit—such as love, joy, peace, patience, kindness, goodness, faithfulness, gentleness, and self-control—we will be empowered to live fruitful and submitted lives unto the Lord and will be an example to others.

This book was written to lay out the simple truth about the Holy Spirit. We need to shake off ignorance concerning the Holy Spirit, His role, His baptism, His gifts, and His function in intercession. It is time for the church of the living God to arise clothed in the dignity and power of the Holy Spirit to reconcile a lost and dying world to Jesus Christ. It is my prayer that reading this book will forever change your life. The truth herein transformed my life over three decades ago, and I continue to hunger and thirst for more of God as I invite the Holy Spirit to reveal Himself to me daily. Be blessed and changed as you read through these pages and allow the Holy Spirit to transform your life through His truth.

Chapter 1

WHO IS THE HOLY SPIRIT?

The Holy Spirit Is God

The Holy Spirit is God! In Genesis 1:1–2 the Bible says, "In the beginning God created the heavens and the earth. Now the earth was formless and empty, darkness was over the surface of the deep, and the Spirit of God was hovering over the waters." Other translations state, "The Spirit of God was moving (hovering, brooding) over the face of the waters" (AMP). This tells us the Holy Spirit was with God from the beginning of time, and He was the creative power source that brought forth God's universe.

> By the word of the Lord were the heavens made, and all their host by the breath of His mouth.
>
> —Psalm 33:6, AMP

The two creative forces that brought forth creation were the Word, and the Spirit of God.[1] John 1:1 says, "In the beginning [before all time] was the Word (Christ), and the Word was with God, and the Word was God Himself" (AMP).

As we've discussed, one of the mysteries about the nature of God is that He is one, yet three persons: the Father, the Son (Jesus), and the Holy Spirit. In Genesis 3:22 the Bible says, "And the Lord God said, Behold, the man has become like one of Us [the Father, Son, and Holy Spirit]" (AMP). It is important to understand that the Holy Spirit is a part of the personhood of God; through the Holy Spirit, God can be everywhere at the same time and know everything. By *person* or *personhood* I mean a being who speaks, listens, and feels—as we do. God is not, however, human (although He did—because He can do anything—come to Earth as a human, as Jesus).

> O Lord, you have searched me and you know me. You know when I sit and when I rise; you perceive my thoughts from afar. You discern my going out and my lying down; you are familiar with all my ways. Before a word is on my tongue you know it completely, O Lord. You hem me in—behind and before; you have laid your hand upon me. Such knowledge is too wonderful for me, too lofty for me to attain. Where can I go from your Spirit? Where can I flee from your presence?
>
> —Psalm 139:1–7

God's wisdom and presence permeate all of creation. God is the living, sovereign King of the universe. David, writer of the psalm above, expressed this notion of an all-encompassing God when he wrote, "Where can I go from your Spirit? Where can I flee from your presence?" God is spirit. He is not confined in a body, and His reality is spiritual. First Timothy 1:17 says, "Now to the King eternal, immortal, invisible, the only God, be honor and glory forever and ever. Amen." In John 4:24 the Word says, "God is a Spirit (a spiritual Being) and those who worship Him must worship Him in spirit and in truth (reality)" (AMP). He is omnipresent, which means He is boundless and free to move and be in all places at all times. He has no limits. He moves and flows without restraint.

> Now the Lord is the Spirit, and where the Spirit of the Lord is, there is freedom.
>
> —2 Corinthians 3:17

We cannot flee from His presence. When we are far from God, He is close to us by His Spirit. In *The Holy Spirit in You*, Derek Prince tells us that "God's presence throughout the universe is His Holy Spirit. God through the Holy Spirit is present everywhere; and through the Holy Spirit, God knows all that is going on in the universe at any time."[2]

The Holy Spirit Gives Ability, Wisdom, and Power

There are many references to the Spirit throughout the Old Testament. In Exodus 35:31, Bezalel was given special talents by the Spirit to devise artistic designs, and to work in gold, silver, and bronze: "And He has filled him with the Spirit of God, with ability and wisdom, with intelligence and understanding, and with knowledge and all craftsmanship" (AMP). When the Lord called Gideon to be a mighty man of strength and courage in order to deliver Israel from the Midianites, Gideon was from the poorest clan in Manasseh and was the youngest and smallest in his father's house. Gideon thought God had made a big mistake choosing him; but we're told in Judges 6:34 that "the Spirit of the Lord clothed Gideon with Himself and took possession of him" (AMP). Samson was also given special gifts by the Spirit. In Judges 13:24–25 the Word says, "The woman gave birth to a boy and named him Samson. He grew and the LORD blessed him, and the Spirit of the LORD began to stir him." This gift grew in magnitude, as we see in Judges 14:6: "And the Spirit of the Lord came mightily upon him" (AMP). When Samuel the prophet anointed Saul as king of Israel, the Bible says in 1 Samuel 10:6, "The Spirit of the Lord will come upon you mightily, and you will show yourself to be a prophet with them; and you will be turned into another man" (AMP). In 1 Samuel 10:10, we're told "the Spirit of God came upon him [Saul] in power, and he joined in their prophesying." The Old Testament prophet Joel tells us, "And afterward, I will pour out my Spirit on all people. Your sons and daughters will prophesy, your old men will dream dreams, your young men will see visions. Even on my servants, both men and women, I will pour out my Spirit in those days" (Joel 2:28–29). This prophecy is specifically referenced (in Acts 2:17–21) as having come true in Peter's time.

As we can see from the scripture mentioned above, the Spirit gave men creative talents and abilities; He empowered leaders who mightily delivered Israel from its enemies and spoke prophecy through the prophets that was specifically fulfilled hundreds and thousands of years later. In 2 Peter 1:21, Peter states, "For prophecy never had its origin in the will of man, but men spoke from God as they were carried along by the Holy Spirit."

The Holy Spirit Is a Person

In his book *The Holy Spirit: Activating God's Power in Your Life*, Billy Graham asserts that the Holy Spirit is a *person* and discusses the following attributes.[3] In John 14, 15, and 16, Jesus spoke of the Holy Spirit as "He." The following are some of the attributes that speak to the Holy Spirit's personhood.

He *speaks*

> He who has an ear, let him hear what the Spirit says to the churches. To him who overcomes, I will give the right to eat from the tree of life, which is in the paradise of God.
>
> —Revelation 2:7

> But the Counselor, the Holy Spirit, whom the Father will send in my name, will teach you all things and will remind you of everything I have said to you.
>
> —John 14:26

> While they were worshiping the Lord and fasting, the Holy Spirit said, "Set apart for me Barnabas and Saul for the work to which I have called them."
>
> —Acts 13:2

You will notice in the Book of Acts there is mention, several times, that the Spirit spoke. When Peter fell into a trance in Joppa while at the home of Simon the tanner, the scripture states, "the Spirit said to him, '...three men are seeking you. Arise therefore, go down and go with them, doubting nothing; for I have sent them'" (Acts 10:19–20, NKJV). At the conversion of the Ethiopian eunuch, "an angel of the Lord said to Philip, 'Go south to the road—the desert road—that goes down from Jerusalem to Gaza.' So he started out, and on his way he met an Ethiopian eunuch... This man had gone to Jerusalem to worship, and on his way home was sitting in his chariot reading the book of Isaiah the prophet. The Spirit told Philip, 'Go to that chariot and stay near it'" (Acts 8:26–29). Phillip had several supernatural encounters that are related in Acts 8:26–40. First an angel appeared to Philip and gave him instruction. Secondly, the Spirit spoke to Philip and gave him instruction. After the eunuch's baptism, the Spirit suddenly took Philip away; he appeared then at Azotus and traveled about preaching the gospel in all the surrounding towns. These are only a few examples of the Holy Spirit speaking to men.

He works on our behalf

> In the same way the Spirit also helps our weakness; for we do not know how to pray as we should, but the Spirit Himself intercedes for us with groanings too deep for words.
>
> —Romans 8:26, NASB

He leads

> For all who are being led by the Spirit of God, these are sons of God.
>
> —Romans 8:14, nasb

He guides

> When the Spirit of truth comes, he will guide you into all the truth, for he will not speak on his own authority, but whatever he hears he will speak, and he will declare to you the things that are to come.
>
> —John 16:13, esv

He brings revelation

> No one knows the thoughts of God except the Spirit of God.
>
> —1 Corinthians 2:11

> This is what we speak, not in words taught us by human wisdom but in words taught by the Spirit.
>
> —1 Corinthians 2:13

He holds us accountable

> Then Peter said, "Ananias, how is it that Satan has so filled your heart that you have lied to the Holy Spirit and have kept for yourself some of the money you received for the land?"
>
> —Acts 5:3

He advises

> And I will ask the Father, and he will give you another Counselor to be with you forever—the Spirit of truth.
>
> —John 14:16–17

> But the Counselor, the Holy Spirit, whom the Father will send in my name, will teach you all things and will remind you of everything I have said to you.
>
> —John 14:26

He teaches

> We have not received the spirit of the world but the Spirit who is from God, that we may understand what God has freely given us. This is what we speak, not in words taught us by human wisdom but in words taught by the Spirit, expressing spiritual truths in spiritual words.
>
> —1 Corinthians 2:12–13

He *glorifies* Jesus

> But when he, the Spirit of truth, comes...He will bring glory to me by taking from what is mine and making it known to you.
>
> —John 16:13–14

The Holy Spirit reveals Jesus through the Word to seekers. He confirms His Word and teaches us truth. When you ask the Holy Spirit to open the Word to you and give you hunger for God, your life starts being transformed.

Evangelist Benny Hinn says the Holy Spirit is a person who can feel, perceive, and respond, and who gets hurt. He has the ability to love and hate, can speak, and has His own will. He is gentle, mighty, and powerful—and longs to have a personal relationship with you![4]

The Holy Spirit has been with God, bringing forth His purposes and prophecies throughout history (His story). He is a real person with a mind and feelings, just like the Father and Son. In *They*

Speak with Other Tongues, John Sherrill summarizes important facts about the Holy Spirit. He writes:

- In the Old and New Testaments both, the Spirit is thought of in terms of action. Words that suggest movement—*fire, wind, breath, rain, dove*—are used to refer to Him. The Spirit is dynamic: He is God in action.
- In the Old Testament there are inferences that the Spirit is personal; in the New Testament this side of Him is stressed. Christ is constantly giving names to the Spirit that describe His shepherding, brooding, caring nature. He calls the Spirit, Guide, Counselor, Comforter, Advocate.
- In both the Old and New Testaments the concept of power and Spirit are closely allied. In the Old Testament the power operates principally through great kings and prophets who lead the nation. In the New Testament the power is now about to be bestowed on the ordinary people who follow Christ.
- In both Testaments, when the Spirit touches human life, personality is transformed.[5]

The Holy Spirit Is the Power of God

From hovering over the waters at Creation to the immaculate conception of Jesus Christ, the Holy Spirit is a power source God granted to man. Indeed, He fueled everything Jesus accomplished in His miraculous ministry. In *Good Morning, Holy Spirit*, Benny Hinn mentions several examples of the Holy Spirit working within men of God and through circumstances to bring forth His power and deliverance for Israel. A few of those examples are as follows:

- When Moses was bringing Israel out of Egypt, the power of God was evidenced in many signs and wonders. The Holy Spirit was the power source behind the wind that divided the Red Sea and all the other miracles in the Book of Exodus.
- The Book of Joshua tells us that Joshua moved in power and might as he led Israel into the Promised Land; this was power given to him by the Holy Spirit.
- In the lives of the Old Testament prophets, David, and other great men of God, the Holy Spirit brought forth the fulfillment of prophecy, empowered David for battle and victory, and brought forth the creative miracles all through the Scripture.
- The Holy Spirit was the power in the life of Jesus. "The Spirit of the LORD is upon Me, Because He has anointed Me to preach the gospel" (Luke 4:18, NKJV).[6]

Additionally—and most notably—the power evidenced in the apostles after the resurrection of Jesus was the Holy Spirit, just as Jesus had promised them. The healings and miraculous signs and wonders performed by Peter and Paul were by the unction and power of the Holy Spirit. They lived and moved and had their being in the Spirit of God.

As you grow in your knowledge and experience with the Holy Spirit, He will become your friend. He desires to commune with you, according to Paul in 2 Corinthians 13:14: "The grace of the Lord Jesus Christ, and the love of God, and the communion of the Holy Spirit be with you" (NKJV). And as you communicate more and more with the Spirit, your life will become alive and ablaze with revelation from His Word. The more you invite the Holy Spirit into your life, the more you will be transformed by His power. From spending time in His presence, you will increase in spiritual power and may have supernatural experiences according to His Word.

THINK ABOUT IT

1. What was your understanding of the Holy Spirit before you started this study?
2. Had you ever considered that the Holy Spirit was present in the Old Testament too?
3. Give examples of the Holy Spirit empowering people in the Old Testament.
4. Give examples of the Holy Spirit's power in the New Testament.
5. Think about what it means to have the Holy Spirit present within you.

Chapter 2

WHAT WAS THE ROLE OF THE HOLY SPIRIT IN THE LIFE OF JESUS?

The story of the birth of Jesus is a wonder conceived in the heart of God. A young Jewish virgin engaged to Joseph, a descendent from the house of King David, is visited in Nazareth by the angel Gabriel. Gabriel tells Mary she is favored and blessed beyond all women; he tells her she will become pregnant by the Holy Spirit and will give birth to a son, whose name will be Jesus, which means "Jehovah is salvation." Gabriel tells Mary that her baby is the son of the Most High.

> Then the angel said to her, The Holy Spirit will come upon you, and the power of the Most High will overshadow you [like a shining cloud]; and so the holy (pure, sinless) Thing (Offspring) which shall be born of you will be called the Son of God.
>
> —Luke 1:35, amp

Jesus' Early Years

When Joseph heard Mary was pregnant, he decided to break their engagement. But another of God's angels appeared to him in a dream and told him not to be afraid to take Mary as his wife. (See Matthew 2:20.) After their marriage, a decree went out from

Caesar Augustus to the entire Roman Empire, requiring all citizens to register in their ancestral city or town. Although they lived in Nazareth, Joseph and Mary traveled to Bethlehem, because Joseph's ancestors were from Bethlehem. Mary was pregnant and due to give birth. Because there was no room for them in the local inn, Joseph and Mary had to spend the night in a stable. It was in this lowly stable that Jesus, the King of the universe, was born by a young mother who laid Him in a manger in swaddling clothes.

Jesus Is Baptized and Empowered by the Holy Spirit

As time passed, John the Baptist, a prophet who predicted and anticipated the coming of Jesus Christ, preached a baptism of repentance and forgiveness of sin in the wilderness near the River Jordan. As Luke tells us, John's message was, "Prepare the way of the Lord; make His beaten paths straight" (Luke 3:4, AMP). John came to prepare the way for Jesus and His ministry. He introduced Jesus as "the Baptizer in the Holy Spirit," meaning that while John baptized people with water as a symbol of having left their old, sin-filled lives behind, those who went further—who knew, followed, and believed in Jesus—would receive a new life with the power they would receive from the Holy Spirit. This was made possible by Jesus.

> I indeed baptize you in (with) water because of repentance [that is, because of your changing your minds for the better, heartily amending your ways, with abhorrence of your past sins]. But He Who is coming after me is mightier than I, Whose sandals I am not worthy or fit to take off or carry; He will baptize you with the Holy Spirit and with fire.
>
> —Matthew 3:11, AMP

John's purpose as the forerunner of Jesus was to bring people to repentance of sin and familiarity with baptism. (Jesus would then eventually baptize His followers with the Holy Spirit and fire.) Out of obedience to a word from God, Jesus came from Galilee to the Jordan to John to be baptized by him. Matthew 3:16 says, "And when Jesus was baptized, He went up at once out of the water; and behold, the heavens were opened, and he [John] saw the Spirit of God descending like a dove and alighting on Him" (AMP).

After Jesus was baptized, He "was led (guided) by the [Holy] Spirit into the wilderness (desert) to be tempted (tested and tried) by the devil" (Matt. 4:1, AMP). After Jesus was tested in the wilderness—and overcame the devil's temptations—He started His ministry in Galilee, where He chose disciples and preached the good news that the kingdom of God was at hand. His miraculous healings and signs and wonders are recorded in the four Gospels (Matthew, Mark, Luke, and John). His life was empowered by the Holy Spirit. He was resurrected from the dead by the Holy Spirit, and He ascended into heaven to sit at the right hand of the Father by the Holy Spirit.

What compelled people to follow Jesus? What made Him different? Jesus moved in extraordinary power that far exceeded what was considered normal. He worked miracles and opened blind eyes and deaf ears. He healed the lame and the lepers and raised the dead. Jesus fed a crowd of five thousand people with just five loaves and two fish. He spoke to the wind and rain, and storms ceased. Jesus took authority over demonic power and cast out demons. A great deal of His ministry was delivering people from the power of the devil and setting the captives free. The power of the Holy Spirit is what allowed Jesus to do these things.

Jesus walked in spiritual authority; He unlocked truths in Scripture the people had never understood. He confounded the religious leaders of the day with His wisdom and understanding of the kingdom of God. The Pharisees hated Him because He carried power and revelation of truth they could not explain. Jesus' proclamation that He was the Christ, the Son of God, ultimately caused the Jewish leaders to crucify Him. However, because of the power of the Holy Spirit, the grave could not hold Him, and He rose from the dead to forever reign in glory.

Jesus Returns to Heaven: He Sends the Holy Spirit

Before Jesus ascended to heaven, He made full provision for all of His disciples (not just the Twelve) to continue the powerful work He had begun. From the following scripture, it is clear Jesus intended for all believers to do the works He did. In John 14:12–17, He says, "I tell you the truth, anyone who has faith in me will do what I have been doing. He will do even greater things than these, because I am going to the Father. And I will do whatever you ask in my name, so that the Son may bring glory to the Father. You may ask me for anything in my name, and I will do it. If you love me, you will obey what I command. And I will ask the Father, and he will give you another Counselor to be with you forever—the Spirit of truth. The world cannot accept him, because it neither sees him nor knows him. But you know him, for he lives with you and will be in you." We know this power to which Jesus refers does not come from human sources but only through the Holy Spirit. Without the Holy Spirit, there is no power for the miraculous.

The purpose of the overview of the beginning of Jesus' life on Earth is to chronicle the role of the Holy Spirit from Jesus' conception to His resurrection from the dead to His ascension. Jesus was empowered by the Spirit throughout His earthly ministry, and He promised His disciples they also would be given the Holy Spirit.

> For the [Holy] Spirit had not yet been given, because Jesus was not yet glorified (raised to honor).
>
> —John 7:39, amp

Before Jesus ascended into heaven, He told His disciples to wait in Jerusalem until they were clothed with power from on high. He told them: "For John baptized with water, but not many days from now you shall be baptized with (placed in, introduced into) the Holy Spirit" (Acts 1:5, AMP). And in Acts 1:8 Jesus says, "But you shall receive power (ability, efficiency, and might) when the Holy Spirit has come upon you, and you shall be My witnesses in Jerusalem and all Judea and Samaria and to the ends (the very bounds) of the earth" (AMP). Before Jesus left His earthly ministry, He made full provision for this power to be given to His followers—by sending us His Spirit. About this He said, "But I tell you the truth: It is for your good that I am going away. Unless I go away, the Counselor will not come to you; but if I go, I will send him to you" (John 16:7).

In order to be evangelists to all the world, we need to receive power from the Holy Spirit. Most of us find it difficult to evangelize in our own backyards. Part of the reason for the lack of power to live and witness for Jesus may be we have not *really* believed that the baptism of the Holy Spirit is for all followers of Jesus—even today. It is easier to believe traditional denominational doctrine, which typically teaches nothing on this subject or teaches that the baptism of Jesus (Holy Spirit) ceased with the death of the first-century apostles.

The Holy Spirit does not dwell within anyone who has not confessed Jesus as Lord and Savior. Romans 10:9–10 tells us, "If you confess with your mouth that Jesus is Lord and believe in your heart that God raised him from the dead, you will be saved. For with the heart one believes and is justified, and with the mouth one confesses and is saved" (ESV). Before we discuss the baptism of the Holy Spirit, let's think about salvation and being born of the Spirit. One must be born again (saved) before one is ready to receive the baptism of the Holy Spirit.

Think About It

1. What does it mean for Jesus to be the Baptizer in the Holy Spirit?

2. In John 14:12–17, Jesus tells us two very important things—that whatever we ask for in His name, He will intercede with God on our behalf, and that He would send someone to be with us in His absence from the world. Have you felt the presence of the Holy Spirit?
3. Do you believe the Lord will answer your prayers and do whatever you ask in His name?
4. Acts 1:8 says that we shall receive power when the Holy Spirit comes. Have you ever had the experience of being filled with this power?

Chapter 3

BEING BORN OF THE SPIRIT

Many Christians are confused about being born of the Spirit (the Holy Spirit becoming present within you at the time of your salvation) and being baptized with the "baptism of Jesus" (being baptized or filled with the Holy Spirit). These are two different experiences. Being born of the Spirit means that at the time you say out loud you believe Jesus is Lord, while simultaneously believing in your heart all you know of Him—that He was conceived by the Holy Spirit, born of the virgin, was crucified and died and then raised from the dead by God—you shall be saved and "receive the Spirit," which welcomes you into the kingdom of God. (The basic requirement for salvation is found in Romans 10:9: "That if you confess with your mouth, 'Jesus is Lord,' and believe in your heart that God raised him from the dead, you will be saved.")

After you are saved, being filled with the Holy Spirit increases your power for living for Jesus and for ministry. In order to gain truth concerning these events, it is necessary to come to God in sincerity and absolute honesty of heart and mind and let the Lord reveal His Word to you. Let's take a look at scriptures that make a distinction between these two occurrences.

DISCIPLES ARE BORN AGAIN AND RECEIVE THE HOLY SPIRIT

The disciples had lived with and followed Jesus for three years. They loved Him and had given their lives to Him (except for Judas), but they did not receive the Holy Spirit until after Jesus rose from the dead. On His resurrection day, after meeting Mary Magdalene at the tomb, Jesus made Himself known to the disciples in His resurrected body. John 20:19–22 tells the story: "Then on that same first day of the week, when it was evening, though the disciples were behind closed doors for fear of the Jews, Jesus came and stood among them and said, Peace to you! So saying, He showed them His hands and His side. And when the disciples saw the Lord, they were filled with joy (delight, exultation, ecstasy, rapture). Then Jesus said to them again, Peace to you! [Just] as the Father has sent Me forth, so I am sending you. And having said this, He breathed on them and said to them, Receive the Holy Spirit!" (AMP). In the New King James, Amplified, New American Standard, and the New International versions of the Bible, this scripture says, "Receive the Holy Spirit." The Holy Spirit was only to come after Jesus had been resurrected from the dead. One of Jesus' first assignments after His resurrection was to breathe on the disciples so they could receive the Holy Spirit. This was the first moment they believed Jesus had been raised from the dead. According to Romans 10:9, this was the time that they were regenerated, or born again, and became new creations in Christ. Second Corinthians 5:17 says, "Therefore, if anyone is in Christ, he is a new creation; the old has gone, the new has come!"

However, Jesus' followers did not receive the baptism of Jesus (in which they were filled with the Holy Spirit) until the day of Pentecost. On that day, their baptism in the Holy Spirit would come after they had tarried in Jerusalem.

Disciples Are Filled (Baptized) with the Holy Spirit

On the day of Pentecost, a group numbering about 120 were in prayer in Jerusalem in an upper room, where they were waiting for the gift Jesus had promised. In Acts 1:4–5 we read, "And while being in their company and eating with them, He commanded them not to leave Jerusalem but to wait for what the Father had promised, Of which [He said] you have heard Me speak. For John baptized with water, but not many days from now you shall be baptized with (placed in, introduced into) the Holy Spirit" (AMP). In Acts 2:1–4 we read, "And when the day of Pentecost had fully come, they were all assembled together in one place, When suddenly there came a sound from heaven like the rushing of a violent tempest blast, and it filled the whole house in which they were sitting. And there appeared to them tongues resembling fire, which were separated and distributed and which settled on each one of them. And they were all filled (diffused throughout their souls) with the Holy Spirit and began to speak in other (different, foreign) languages (tongues), as the Spirit kept giving them clear and loud expression [in each tongue in appropriate words]" (AMP).

It is clear from Scripture that Jesus breathed on the disciples and told them to receive the Holy Spirit on the day of His resurrection, which occurred before the day of Pentecost, when the people in the upper room were filled, baptized, and empowered with the Holy Spirit. When they were filled with the Holy Spirit, they spoke in tongues as the Spirit gave them the ability to do so. Pentecost was the fulfillment and promise of Acts 1:4–5. Derek Prince explains, "The Holy Spirit descended from heaven in person, in the form of a mighty wind, filled each one of them individually, and gave each one a new and supernatural utterance in a language they had never learned."[7] Speaking in tongues is a supernatural manifestation of the baptism of the Holy Spirit, and it is one of the gifts of the Holy Spirit that will be discussed later. The next mention in Scripture about receiving the Holy Spirit is in Acts 8.

Samaritan Believers Receive the Holy Spirit

When the apostles heard that Samaria had received the word of God, they sent Peter and John to them. (See Acts 8:14.) In Acts 8:15–17 we read, "When they arrived, they prayed for them that they might receive the Holy Spirit, because the Holy Spirit had not yet come upon any of them; they had simply been baptized into the name of the Lord Jesus. Then Peter and John placed their hands on them, and they received the Holy Spirit." In this scripture, we see the Samaritans had given their lives to Jesus when Philip preached the good news. They were baptized in water and had been born again, but the Holy Spirit had not yet come upon them. At the time of salvation, the Holy Spirit comes to permanently dwell in us. With the laying on of hands by Peter and John, the Samaritans were filled (baptized) with the Holy Spirit. These were two separate experiences.

Cornelius's Household Receives Salvation and the Holy Spirit

Cornelius, a centurion, was a righteous and God-fearing man who had a visitation from an angel of God who told him to send men to Joppa to bring back a man called Peter. (Read Cornelius's story in Acts 10.) In the meantime Peter, while in Joppa, had fallen into a trance; later, when he was pondering the meaning of the vision, the Spirit told him that three men were looking for him and he should go with them. Peter went with the men to Cornelius's house. There he found the centurion's close friends and relatives gathered. Peter told them the story of Jesus and how the Holy Spirit had anointed Him with power to work miracles, heal the sick, and take authority over the power of the devil. While Peter was telling them that everyone who believed in Jesus would receive forgiveness of sins through His name, the Holy Spirit came upon on all who heard the message. Acts 10:44–48 reads, "While Peter was still speaking these words, the Holy Spirit came on all who heard the message. The circumcised believers who had come with Peter were astonished that the gift of the Holy Spirit had been poured out even on the Gentiles. For they heard them speaking in tongues and praising God. Then Peter said, 'Can anyone keep these people from being baptized with water? They have received the Holy Spirit just as we have.' So he ordered that they be baptized in the name of Jesus Christ. Then they asked Peter to stay with them for a few days."

Cornelius and his household received the good news about Jesus and immediately responded in their hearts, resulting in their receiving the gift of the Holy Spirit and speaking in tongues before they were water baptized. Once Peter saw that they had received the Holy Spirit just as those in Jerusalem and Samaria had, he water baptized them in the name of Jesus Christ.

Ephesian Believers Are Filled with the Holy Spirit

When Paul arrived at Ephesus, he found some disciples and asked them if they had received the Holy Spirit when they believed in Jesus. (See Acts 19:1–2.) They reported that they had not heard there was a Holy Spirit. Paul further learned they had been baptized into John's baptism, which was a baptism of repentance. He explained that John taught there was One to come after him, who was Jesus. Upon hearing this truth, the Ephesians were baptized into the name of Jesus. Following that baptism, Paul placed his hands on them, and the Holy Spirit came upon them. Let's look at Acts 19:5–6: "On hearing this, they were baptized into the name of the Lord Jesus. When Paul placed his hands on them, the Holy Spirit came on them, and they spoke in tongues and prophesied."

In this scripture, we see Ephesian believers who understood

John's teaching and were baptized by him; they were seeking the kingdom of God. When Paul arrived, they were taught about Jesus and also believed. After their water baptism, Paul laid his hands on them, and they were filled with the Holy Spirit, as manifested by their speaking in tongues and prophesying. Again, we see two separate experiences.

A person is born again as soon as he confesses Jesus as Lord and the Holy Spirit comes in to permanently dwell there. John 3 tells a story about Nicodemus, a Pharisee who came by night to seek Jesus. John 3:3–5 says, "In reply Jesus declared, 'I tell you the truth, no one can see the kingdom of God unless he is born again.' 'How can a man be born when he is old?' Nicodemus asked. 'Surely he cannot enter a second time into his mother's womb to be born!' Jesus answered, 'I tell you the truth, no one can enter the kingdom of God unless he is born of water and the Spirit.'" This scripture suggests that when we are born again we receive the Holy Spirit. Water baptism should follow our conversion experience. There is no mention of the baptism of Jesus or being filled with the Holy Spirit in this passage. The baptism in the Holy Spirit follows our "born again, receiving Jesus as Lord" experience. (However, Cornelius's experience was different. He received the baptism of the Holy Spirit and was later baptized in water.)

We have discussed the two distinct experiences of being born again (saved, converted) and the baptism of Jesus (being filled or baptized in the Holy Spirit). Now let's take a look at what Scripture says about the baptism of Jesus.

Think About It

1. Did you realize that to receive the Holy Spirit at the time of your salvation was a different experience from being baptized in the Holy Spirit (i.e., the baptism of the Holy Spirit, or baptism of Jesus)?

2. Had you considered that, like you, the disciples actually became born again?
3. There are numerous accounts throughout Acts of believers being baptized in the Holy Spirit, including the 120 who were baptized in the Holy Spirit on the day of Pentecost in the upper room. (See Acts 2:1–4.) Do you have a new understanding of these scriptures? Why?
4. What have you learned about the difference between being born again and being baptized in the Holy Spirit?"

Chapter 4

BAPTISM of JESUS/BAPTISM of the HOLY SPIRIT

Jesus, the Baptizer in the Spirit, is mentioned in all four Gospels.

> I baptize you with water for repentance. But after me will come one who is more powerful than I, whose sandals I am not fit to carry. He will baptize you with the Holy Spirit and with fire.
>
> —Matthew 3:11

> I have baptized you with water, but He will baptize you with the Holy Spirit.
>
> —Mark 1:8, AMP

> John answered them all by saying, I baptize you with water; but He Who is mightier than I is coming, the strap of Whose sandals I am not fit to unfasten. He will baptize you with the Holy Spirit and with fire.
>
> —Luke 3:16, AMP

> And I did not know Him nor recognize Him, but He Who sent me to baptize in (with) water said to me, Upon Him Whom you shall see the Spirit descend and

> remain, that One is He Who baptizes with the Holy Spirit.
>
> —JOHN 1:33, AMP

The Holy Spirit powered Jesus' ministry on Earth, and Jesus promised the Holy Spirit would be given to His disciples when He had been glorified.

In John 7:37–39 the Word says the following: "If any man is thirsty, let him come to Me and drink! He who believes in Me [who cleaves to and trusts in and relies on Me] as the Scripture has said, From his innermost being shall flow [continuously] springs and rivers of living water. But He was speaking here of the Spirit, Whom those who believed (trusted, had faith) in Him were afterward to receive. For the [Holy] Spirit had not yet been given, because Jesus was not yet glorified (raised to honor)" (AMP).

If you notice in verse 37, the thirsty are invited to come to Him (Jesus) to drink. Those who thirst and hunger for a living God long for something more from their relationship with Jesus. Status quo religious experience is not enough! Their longing for God will cause them to "cleave to and trust in and rely on" Him *until* springs and rivers of living water flow from their inmost parts. This scripture describes the outflow of the baptism of Jesus that is mentioned in the Gospels.

When you are thirsty and hungry for more of God, you start looking for answers and knowledge that will take you into a deeper relationship with Him. You will find yourself spending more time reading your Bible. You start to pray more; you will cry out, asking for more and more wisdom and revelation and knowledge of Him. You will hunger to go deeper and deeper in your relationship with Jesus. As your thirst and hunger intensify, the Holy Spirit starts to give you revelation concerning the baptism of Jesus, or baptism in the Holy Spirit. Becoming hungry for a deeper relationship with Jesus causes Christians to seek this baptism in the Holy Spirit.

Hunger for God causes us to go beyond denominational

doctrine, which usually teaches that the baptism in the Holy Spirit was only for the early church and is not something we should expect to experience today. But the more you study, the more you will start to question what you have been taught in the past. If you have been taught that the baptism of Jesus "passed away," you will have much to unlearn before you can move forward. Getting rid of any negative, preconceived mind-sets against the baptism of the Holy Spirit will allow you more quickly to act in faith and receive this wonderful blessing and empowerment. You will start having divine appointments, meeting other Christians who have received the baptism in the Holy Spirit, and they will be able to explain further the baptism of Jesus.

How to Open Up to Receive the Holy Spirit

In order for us to receive the Holy Spirit, there are some requirements that we must first fulfill.[8]

1. Repent and be baptized

Before we start asking to receive the Holy Spirit, we need to repent and be baptized. In Acts 2:38, "Peter replied, 'Repent and be baptized, every one of you, in the name of Jesus Christ for the forgiveness of your sins. And you will receive the gift of the Holy Spirit.'" Before we can receive the Holy Spirit, we must repent and be baptized. The Spirit, in His grace, woos us and guides us and gives the ability to turn our lives over to God. This process of conversion and salvation leads us to repentance and water baptism. Through water baptism, we identify with Jesus' death, burial, and resurrection.

2. Ask for and seek the Holy Spirit

John 14:14–17 says, "You may ask me for anything in my name, and I will do it. If you love me, you will obey what I command. And I will ask the Father, and he will give you another Counselor to be with you forever—the Spirit of truth. The world cannot accept him, because it neither sees him nor knows him. But you know him, for he lives with you and will be in you." Asking is an important part of receiving the baptism of the Holy Spirit. The Word says we do not *have* because we do not *ask*. In Luke 11:9–13 Jesus says the following: "So I say to you, Ask and keep on asking and it shall be given you; seek and keep on seeking and you shall find; knock and keep on knocking and the door shall be opened to you. For everyone who asks and keeps on asking receives; and he who seeks and keeps on seeking finds; and to him who knocks and keeps on knocking, the door shall be opened. What father among you, if his son asks for a loaf of bread, will give him a stone; or if he asks for a fish, will instead of a fish give him a serpent? Or if he asks for an egg, will give him a scorpion? If you then, evil as you are, know how to give good gifts [gifts that are to their advantage] to your children, how much more will your heavenly Father give the Holy Spirit to those who ask and continue to ask Him!" (AMP). We see from this scripture that asking is an important part of the process of receiving the Holy Spirit and sometimes we have to continue to ask *until we receive.*

3. Thirst for Him

John 7:37–39 states, "'If anyone is thirsty, let him come to me and drink. Whoever believes in me, as the Scripture has said, streams of living water will flow from within him.' By this he meant the Spirit, whom those who believed in him were later to receive. Up to that time the Spirit had not been given, since Jesus had not yet been glorified." As this verse says, Jesus was making reference to the arrival of the Spirit *after His ascension*. If you are thirsty for God, you desire more of Him. You need more of Him than you have now. You are not satisfied with your current spiritual experience. You are compelled by the Spirit to seek more.

Jesus is the Baptizer in the Holy Spirit, so you must come to Him and ask that He baptize you in the Spirit. When you drink deeply of the water of life that Jesus offers, streams of living water will overflow out of you to others.

My Story of Hunger for God

It was not until I was born again that I started to hunger for more of God. I experienced "marketplace evangelism" at its best prior to my salvation. I met a young woman where I worked who *knew Jesus* and who talked about Him constantly. It was through my relationship with Linda that I became hungry and thirsty for the living God. Hunger for God led me from my salvation experience to the *baptism of Jesus.* Here is my story.

I was gloriously saved and gave my life to Christ in a little blue Volkswagen on a cold winter's night around midnight on February 3, 1972. A powerful transformation started in my life at the time of my conversion: my life became filled with light and love. I had been raised in a Christian home and attended church three times a week all of my life, but when I went to college and got away from home I started to question the teachings of my church. That congregation was made up of precious people who loved God and studied the Word, but a lot of the New Testament was not believed to be true for today. For instance, the church taught that the baptism in the Holy Spirit and the gifts of the Holy Spirit all passed away with the deaths of the apostles; therefore, we had no need for those experiences in the church today. Many other teachings did not line up with what I thought were clear principles in the Bible, so I began my own quest for *truth.* In my quest for truth, I got off the path to God. I was on a slippery slope headed for destruction when the Lord's love and mercy snatched me off a sure path to ruin. I had been playing games with God for a long time when I experienced an earthquake with a magnitude of 4.5 in Memphis, Tennessee, in the summer of 1971, which forever changed my life. At the time of the quake, albeit not a major one, I remember falling on my face on the floor and crying out to God, asking Him to reveal Himself to me.

Soon after praying this prayer, I got fired from my job during the cutbacks and layoffs of that summer. Shortly after roaming the streets of Memphis looking for a job, I landed one as a secretary at BlueCross/BlueShield. Working two desks down was a woman who was like a breath of fresh air in the office. Linda was beautiful, had a radiant smile, and talked about Jesus *all* the time. Every day we would go on break together, and all she talked about was Jesus. I could not believe what I was hearing. She was in *love* with *Him*. I thought this was so strange. Her husband was a marine in Vietnam, she had a baby her husband had never seen (born shortly after he left), and she radiated the love and peace of God. As I hung out with her day after day, she never stopped talking about Jesus. She made me hungry and thirsty for something more in my empty life. Linda had also been baptized in the Holy Spirit and talked about supernatural healings, praying in the Spirit (tongues), and all kinds of things that were in the Bible, although I had been taught not to believe these particular things. The godly influence of this young woman's example caused me to become sickened with my life as it was.

On February 3, 1972, I went to Memphis State University's campus to hear a lecture by Landon Saunders. He was and is a well-respected man of faith who taught a powerful message that penetrated my heart. I felt a sense of destiny while sitting in that large auditorium, not knowing I would make a decision in the next few hours would change my life forever.

I drove to our apartment complex not far from campus on that freezing cold winter's night and sat in my little Volkswagen for two hours. Our neighbor's wolfhound stared in the window as I sat there making the most important decision of my life. This was the first time I had ever heard the voice of the Spirit clearly and without question. He said a couple of things I will always remember. He told me my days were numbered due to the precarious life I had been living and that if I didn't commit my life to Him, my time would be cut short. The second thing He said was that my husband would end up leaving me due to my commitment to Christ. This was terrifying to me since Andy had been my childhood sweetheart, and I loved him better than life itself. The Lord also told me I needed to count the cost! Around midnight on February 3, I surrendered my life to Jesus and asked Him to save my lost soul after spending two hours "counting the cost." I got out of the car and walked up the steps and through the door of our apartment and was changed forevermore.

My newfound love affair with Jesus altered my life completely. I had never been a particularly good student in my undergraduate studies, and I could have cared less about reading anything, textbooks or otherwise. I was a night student at Memphis State University (now Memphis University), and I was limping along through college before my salvation, probably partially due to my lifestyle. After Jesus took hold of my life, my grades went from Cs and Ds to As; in some cases, I had the highest grade in the class. I eventually completed master's and doctorate degrees with almost straight As. All of a sudden I wanted to gain knowledge and understanding about *everything*, so I read constantly. I became a prolific reader and have remained so until this day. My world opened up to many new horizons through my quest for knowledge.

As I grew in my knowledge of the Word and sought the Lord with all my strength, I started to hunger for more. Linda, my friend at work, gave me a small book titled *They Speak with Other Tongues* by John Sherrill, but I was terrified to read it. I thought the information in the book could not be true, because the church I grew up in did not believe such things and thought such teaching was heresy. But my hunger for more of God and a deeper relationship with Him continued to grow.

My husband and I graduated from college and moved back to our small hometown in 1974, and I brought the little book with me. As I started to meet Christians in the community, everyone I met had just been baptized in the Holy Spirit. These were the days of the Jesus movement and the outpouring of the Holy Spirit. The more I hung out with these newly baptized Christians, the more I thirsted for what they had. On June 2, 1974, after reading *They Speak with Other Tongues* and Pat Boone's book *A New Song*, I cried out to Jesus to baptize me in His Spirit.

I remember kneeling beside my bed and lifting my hands to the Lord, which was an uncommon thing for me. Up until that time, I had never had a thought of kneeling before God, and it was not something I had witnessed before. I prayed and asked Him to please baptize me in His Spirit, and I clearly heard His voice in my spirit say, "You care too much about what your husband thinks, what your parents think, and you are afraid you will be excommunicated from your church." So I sat there and pondered these words for some time, and then got up and went about my day. I knew that if I wanted to go on with God into deeper spiritual waters, I had to go beyond caring what my husband, parents, and the church of my childhood thought about this experience called the baptism in the Spirit.

The next morning when my husband left for work, I knelt down once again to seek God for the baptism of the Spirit. My hunger for more of God had bought me to a point that it didn't matter what anyone thought about my quest for a deeper relationship with the Lord. I remember saying to Jesus on June 3, 1974, "I don't care if my husband leaves or if my parents disown me or if I am excommunicated from my church. I want all that You have for my life." As I lifted my hands to the Lord, it felt like He was pouring warm oil on me from the top of my fingertips to the bottom of my feet. I sat transfixed in the presence of the Lord and started to sing a simple, short song in tongues (the Spirit). I am not sure how many hours I sat transfixed in His presence, but I eventually had to get up and go on with my day. I worked around the house and ran errands, and I kept singing this simple little song throughout the day until bedtime.

The next day as I sat down to worship the Lord and to seek His face, I opened my mouth and my new prayer language (praying in tongues, praying in the Spirit) started to pour forth from my "innermost being." The baptism of Jesus took me to a new level of hunger for God and into a new dimension of revelation of the Word and understanding of the gifts of the Holy Spirit. My prayer life became exponentially more powerful, and I started to grow in a deeper knowledge and revelation of God. My relationship with the Lord became stronger and more vibrant, even as tensions started to build with my husband, opening the door to turbulent days ahead. Through hunger for more of God, my life now had a firm foundation on which to stand, and God had become my rock and salvation. Without spiritual strength and a love affair with Jesus, I could never have made it through the difficult years that were coming.

Ask the Lord to Baptize You in the Holy Spirit

If you are not born again and you believe the Holy Spirit is convicting you that Jesus is Lord and that God raised Him from the dead, then ask Jesus to come into your heart and life and save your soul. Ask Him to make all things new in your life and renounce your old life.

A Salvation Prayer

> *Father, I come to You to confess I believe Jesus Christ is the Son of God. I believe that He was born of the Virgin Mary, was crucified and rose from the dead, and ascended into heaven and sits on the right hand of God the Father. I ask You to forgive me of my sins and wash me whiter than snow. Change my life and redeem me to serve and love You with all my mind, soul, heart, spirit, and body all the days of my life. I invite You to come in and take control of my life and to make all things new. In Jesus' name I pray.*

If you are saved and born again, and have carefully read the first four chapters of this book and researched the Scripture, you may be ready to ask Jesus to baptize you in the Holy Spirit. If you are hungry for a deeper relationship with God, then stop right now and ask Jesus to baptize you in the Holy Spirit. Simply pray from your heart and ask Him to come into your life in a deeper measure.

A PRAYER FOR THE BAPTISM OF THE HOLY SPIRIT

> *Lord, I come to You to seek Your face with all my heart, soul, mind, and spirit. I ask you to forgive me of all of my sins. [Ask the Lord to uncover any sin you need to repent of and release it to Him.] I hunger for more of You, and I long for a deeper, more intimate relationship with You. Jesus, I ask You to baptize me in the Holy Spirit with the evidence of speaking in tongues, just as You did for the disciples in the Book of Acts and as you have done for believers throughout the ages. I believe Your Word is true, that Jesus is the Baptizer in the Holy Spirit, and that it is for the church today. So Lord, I invite You to come and powerfully pour out Your Spirit upon me. In Jesus' name I pray.*

Quietly wait in His presence. You may feel a warm heat flood your body. It may feel like warm oil being poured out upon you. The presence of the Lord may descend upon you, and you may experience the cloud of His glory. You may experience a variety of unique manifestations of the Spirit. For all of us it is different and uniquely designed to bless us, empower us, and to draw us near. God probably never does the same thing twice. You may hear unusual words in your thinking. Just as you think in English or your native language, you may start to hear different words, unknown words to you—an unknown language, or "tongue." In faith, open your mouth and start to speak the words you are hearing. If you only receive a few words initially, in faith speak the words the Holy Spirit has given you. I initially only received about ten words of a simple song, but I sang that song until the Lord poured out upon me my prayer language. If you do not receive the baptism, continue to ask and seek *until* you do receive. Ask the Lord why, and He will speak to you.

Obstacles to Receiving the Baptism in the Holy Spirit

In his book *The Walk of the Spirit—The Walk of Power: The Vital Role of Praying in Tongues*, Dave Roberson says that receiving the Holy Spirit is a simple thing, but the devil tries to complicate the process.[9] Maybe you have prayed for the baptism in the Spirit but something seems to be blocking your receiving. Roberson gives some scriptural truth and guidelines that may be helpful in your breakthrough. This is an excellent book, and I recommend that you read his book for insight into the power of praying in the Spirit. He gives the following reasons why people struggle to receive the baptism in the Spirit.

1. Strongholds of the mind

The devil will use negative teachings you have learned about speaking in tongues. "A mental stronghold is a system of thoughts empowered by a person's emotions. This system has been created by a lifetime of faulty reasonings and thought patterns that block the mind from cooperating with God's truth."[10] Many denominations teach that tongues aren't for today. Whatever faulty teaching has been learned, truth can break through. A spirit of denominationalism keeps you bound to the teaching, or lack thereof, of your church, rather than pressing through to the truth in the Scripture.

2. "I'm not good enough to receive the Spirit"

Some people believe they must be free of all deeds of the flesh, such as smoking, drinking, or cursing. They believe they must be sanctified first, yet never have the power to rid themselves of the sin that so easily besets them. But the Bible says it is through *the Spirit* that we have the power to rid ourselves of the deeds of the flesh (sin). When you are saved, God takes out the old nature and creates a new nature in you. It is the new righteous nature that God uses as the reason for baptizing you in the Holy Spirit.[11] The work of recreation has been done, and you are now ready for the Holy Spirit to infill you. To accomplish the work of sanctification, the Holy Spirit wants to "create a supernatural language of tongues on the inside of your spirit" to help you pray without ceasing.[12] As Roberson so powerfully says, "The moment you give utterance to those words and start praying in tongues, you walk into a divine classroom. Standing at the chalkboard is none other than the Master Teacher, the Holy Spirit. He has come into your life to teach, empower, edify, and sanctify."[13]

3. "I don't have to speak in tongues to be filled with the Holy Spirit"

Many people believe they can receive the baptism of the Spirit without evidence of speaking in tongues. The supernatural language can be released into your spirit, but it does not flow from your mouth because of unbelief. The devil tries hard to keep you bound by believing that speaking in tongues is not important and not necessary. People who believe that way don't understand the power God wants to release in their lives through their supernatural language.

4. "I'm waiting for the Holy Spirit to make me speak"

Some people are waiting for the Holy Spirit to move on them and make them speak, when in fact He is waiting on them to receive and give utterance to the language He has released within their spirits. He creates the language and we release in praying. In

Acts 2:4 we're told, "All of them were filled with the Holy Spirit and began to speak in other tongues as the *Spirit enabled them*" (emphasis added). We must press on through until the words come. Strongholds block us from yielding our tongue to the utterance of the language.

If you have struggled to receive the baptism in the Holy Spirit, keep pressing in. If you have only received a few words in a tongue, then in faith offer those few words up in prayer until the Holy Spirit gives you more. As you worship and love the Lord with what He has given you, your faith will be strengthened and your prayer language will increase.

When you are baptized in the Holy Spirit with the manifestation of speaking in tongues, this language becomes a powerful prayer language if you exercise it in faith. The more you use what you have, the more your prayer language will grow. Praying in the Holy Spirit opens a door that will take you from prayer into intercession.

Think About It

1. What role does "asking and seeking" more of God play in preparing your heart to receive the Holy Spirit?
2. What are your thoughts (or fears) about asking Jesus to baptize you in the Holy Spirit?
3. Are you ready to ask Jesus to baptize you in the Spirit? If you are not ready, what do you think is holding you back?

Chapter 5

PRAYING IN THE SPIRIT: A DOOR FROM PRAYER TO INTERCESSION

PRAYING IN TONGUES for your personal edification is a way to build faith. As your faith is built up within your spirit, you are able to grow in prayer and intercession and have faith to believe for healing and miracles. Your life becomes empowered; you have the ability to uncover and fight the devil's schemes in your life and overcome him in the name of Jesus. The more you pray in tongues, the more you are praying God's perfect will for your life and family. You are praying the mysteries of God's plan over people's lives, situations, and circumstances, over governments and nations.

Roberson says, "So when the Holy Spirit creates His supernatural language in you, those tongues originate way down deep in your spiritual mind, which lies within your physical mind. This explains the fact that when the Holy Spirit speaks, it is not a surface speaking. It comes from the depths of that spiritual mind and bursts outwardly into your intellect. That's why if you don't let the tongues come out of your mouth those supernatural words will bypass your mouth and drift up to your thoughts, and you'll 'hear' the tongues in your natural mind."[14] As we exercise this divine gift, we start tapping into the supernatural power of the Spirit. In Jeremiah 33:1, 3, we're told that God spoke to the prophet

Jeremiah: "The word of the Lord came to him...'Call to me and I will answer you and tell you great and unsearchable things you do not know.'" The Spirit starts downloading information, strategies, plans, and direction supernaturally as we pray in the Spirit. We have the privilege of hooking into the unfathomable power of God by praying in the Spirit. If we would take seriously the instruction to pray without ceasing and to pray in the Spirit at all times, our lives would be transformed.

Now let's take a look at the difference between speaking in tongues and praying in the Spirit.

Speaking in Tongues—Praying in the Spirit

As mentioned in the previous chapter, speaking in tongues—often referred to as praying in tongues or the Spirit (languages other than your native tongue)—leads to a door that will take your prayer life from basic prayer into powerful intercession directed by the Holy Spirit. In Romans 8:26–27, Paul emphasizes the necessity of the direction of the Holy Spirit in prayer: "So too the [Holy] Spirit comes to our aid and bears us up in our weakness; for we do not know what prayer to offer nor how to offer it worthily as we ought, but the Spirit Himself goes to meet our supplication and pleads in our behalf with unspeakable yearnings and groanings too deep for utterance. And He Who searches the hearts of men knows what is in the mind of the [Holy] Spirit [what His intent is], because the Spirit intercedes and pleads [before God] in behalf of the saints according to and in harmony with God's will" (AMP).

When it comes to prayer, most of us are weak and have difficulty knowing what to pray. But God has sent His Holy Spirit to help us in our weakness. The Holy Spirit can move in us and does the praying through us. One way this takes place is through praying in the Holy Spirit, that is, using our prayer language (or speaking in tongues). He will guide, direct, and strengthen us during prayer.

As we've seen, Jesus provided His followers with the Holy Spirit, which opens us up to supernatural power and a higher dimension of prayer. Yet, traditional denominations view praying in the Spirit as a strange or unusual spiritual phenomenon. Rather than embrace the Holy Spirit and seek revelation of the scripture that so often speaks of the baptism of Jesus, the baptism of the Holy Spirit, and speaking in tongues (in the Spirit), this supernatural experience is disregarded as unimportant. Jesus expected the baptism of the Holy Spirit to be the next step in spiritual experience after salvation, yet most Christians have little or no understanding or knowledge about the Holy Spirit or His baptism. (See Acts 2:4.)

The New International Version says "the Spirit himself intercedes for us with groans that words cannot express" (Rom. 8:26). Intercessory prayer comes forth from the Holy Spirit through sounds that cannot be expressed in words. In Isaiah 66:8 we're told: "As soon as Zion travailed, she also brought forth her sons" (NASB). Without prayer and spiritual labor, no real growth or change will come forth in the church or our personal lives. Paul also mentions he travailed in prayer and intercession until Christ was formed in the church in Galatians. (See Galatians 4:19.) Intercessory prayer is referred to as being like the pains of childbirth.

In Jude 20–21, the scripture says, "But you, beloved, build yourselves up [founded] on your most holy faith [make progress, rise like an edifice higher and higher], praying in the Holy Spirit; Guard and keep yourselves in the love of God; expect and patiently wait for the mercy of our Lord Jesus Christ (the Messiah)—[which will bring you] unto life eternal" (AMP). In other words, praying in the Holy Spirit is a way to build up your faith and your own spirit. In 1 Corinthians 14:2, we learn, "For one who speaks in an [unknown] tongue speaks not to men but to God, for no one understands or catches his meaning, because in the [Holy] Spirit he utters secret truths and hidden things [not obvious to the understanding]" (AMP). Verse 4 continues, "He who speaks in a [strange] tongue edifies and improves himself, but he who prophesies [interpreting the divine will and purpose and teaching with inspiration] edifies and improves the church and promotes growth [in Christian wisdom, piety, holiness, and happiness]." First Corinthians 14:2 in the New American Standard Version similarly says, "But in his spirit he speaks mysteries."

We can see from the above scriptures that praying in the Spirit edifies and strengthens us in our faith and our spirit. When praying in tongues, you are praising God, praying the perfect will of God, and praying with power. You have no idea what you are praying, but the Holy Spirit is uttering secret truths and mysteries. It is important Christians access all the power available to them to fight the wiles of the devil. One of the reasons Christians may struggle with so many addictions and temptations is because they have refused to believe the baptism in the Holy Spirit is for today *and* because they have failed to seek Jesus earnestly for His empowerment through the baptism in the Spirit.

The pressures of life are overwhelming at times, and one way to stay strong in the midst of out-of-control circumstances is to pray in the Spirit. When you have been baptized in the Holy Spirit, you can "pray without ceasing." Pray with your mind and understanding, and when you have prayed all you know to pray, then shift into your prayer language. The more you pray in the Spirit and exercise this marvelous gift, the more the gift will grow and the more your capacity for intercession will grow.

DIFFERENCE BETWEEN THE GIFT OF TONGUES AND PRAYING IN THE SPIRIT

Before we go further, the difference between the gift of tongues (which is one of the gifts of the Holy Spirit) and the prayer language itself needs to be explained. The gift of speaking in tongues is explained in 1 Corinthians 14:13–15. Paul says, "For this reason anyone who speaks in a tongue should pray that he may interpret what he says. For if I pray in a tongue, my spirit prays, but my mind is unfruitful...I will sing with my spirit, but I will also sing with my mind." Verses 18–19 continue, "I thank God that I speak in tongues more than all of you. But in the church I would rather speak five intelligible words to instruct others than ten thousand words in a tongue." Verse 22 says: "Tongues, then, are a sign, not for believers but for unbelievers; prophecy, however, is for believers." Paul explains an order of a meeting of believers to include the following, saying, "What then shall we say, brothers? When you come together, everyone has a hymn, or a word of instruction, a revelation, a tongue or an interpretation. All of these must be done for the strengthening of the church. If anyone speaks in a tongue, two—or at the most three—should speak, one at a time, and someone must interpret. If there is no interpreter, the speaker should keep quiet in the church and speak to himself and God" (1 Cor. 14:26–28).

What we glean from these passages is the difference between the gift of tongues (the language) and the supernatural message (interpretation of tongues) given by the Holy Spirit to the body of believers who have come together. If someone speaks a word in tongues in a public meeting, he needs to be prepared to interpret the word he has delivered. *This* gift is called "interpretation of tongues" and is another of the gifts of the Spirit. When a tongue is "delivered" in a meeting, there should also be the gifting and faith for the interpretation of the word. (The gift of speaking in tongues and interpretation will be further explained in chapter 6.)

When Paul refers to praying in tongues, he means the spirit is praying. When you are praying in tongues, you are praying in the Holy Spirit and praying, as the Bible says, "secret things" and "hidden truth." When praying in the Holy Spirit, you are hooked up to the eternal power source, who knows all things and sees and understands all things. Praying in the Spirit is one door that takes you into intercession—deeper, more powerful prayer spoken (and groaned) by the Holy Spirit on your behalf *in God's presence.* You are praying the perfect will of God and the mind of Christ when praying in the Spirit; your spirit is speaking mysteries. What more powerful way should we pray?

As you grow and mature, it is important to move into the higher and deeper realms of the Spirit. Exercise your prayer language and pray in tongues often. By doing so you are stirring up the Spirit within. Seek His face and spiritual anointing will increase. Jude 20 says to "build yourselves up in your most holy faith and pray in the Holy Spirit." As you pray in the Spirit, the Lord will impart even more revelation of the Word. You may receive greater vision and strategy to implement personal vision. The supernatural faith to step out and through new doors and gates may be conveyed. You will find yourself; you'll have "healing in your wings" and will begin to soar to new heights. The more you activate your prayer language by praying in the Spirit, the more you will experience your prayer life moving into deeper realms of intercession.

PRAYER THAT LEADS TO INTERCESSION

Prayer allows you to communicate directly with God about things that concern you. Personal devotion increases as you seek God, asking to hunger and thirst for righteousness. The more you grow in prayer, the more you hunger for more of God. You will have as much of God as you desire. You pray to the degree you have hunger. As you grow and mature in your relationship and devotion, the Holy Spirit will take you deeper in the knowledge of Jesus and into a more powerful, effective prayer life.

Spiritual growth requires exercise and effort and prayer—and prayer must become a priority. If prayer is to grow and flourish in your life, it must be nurtured and cultivated to become effective. Such prayer is work and requires a time commitment. If you are serious about the things of God, you will become serious about prayer.

Prayer is rooted in passion and faith. We stir up our faith as we pray. When we add the dimension of praying in the Spirit (tongues), our passion and faith intensify, and we become preoccupied with prayer and advancing the kingdom of God. Faith thrives in an atmosphere of prayer; it grabs hold of the power of God and pulls down blessings from heaven. Faith believes, visualizes the answer, receives, appropriates, manifests, and takes hold of the promises of God.[15]

As we move into an understanding of intercession, James Goll's book *The Lost Art of Intercession* becomes an important resource. Goll brings great insight into an understanding of intercession and the power thereof.[16] This is a must-read for people who are eager to move into the deeper dimensions of prayer through intercession.

As we grow in prayer and start exercising our faith by praying in the Spirit, our prayer life starts to shift into a higher spiritual realm. We will sense we are stepping over into a deeper level of prayer. You will not find in the Scripture the terms *intercession* or *the gift of intercession*. Goll says, "Nowhere is intercession termed a 'gift' or 'grace.' Why? Because it is a *privilege* and household duty of every priest in God's Kingdom of priests and kings. It is what you were reborn to do!"[17] Will you join Him on this road less traveled and become a spiritual adventurer who will search and excavate for lost spiritual treasures?

Let's ask the question, What is intercession? In Numbers 16, Aaron stood in the gap with a censor with fire from the altar and incense and went through the camp of Israel to "stand between the dead and the living" (v. 48, NASB). A classic definition of an intercessor is "one who stands in the gap for another." But this takes a powerful—and fearless—faith.

God wants to remove from you the fear that rejects and avoids the supernatural. The church has grown lukewarm and passionless as she has rejected the Holy Spirit and His power. Moving into intercession requires a choice to move into deeper realms of glory with the Lord. The choice is yours. Do you want to go? Are you willing to stand in the gap for others, for nations and kingdoms and governments?

The spirit of intercession (you will not find this term in the

Scriptures, as mentioned earlier) is compelling and can be overwhelming as it can take you into deep, groaning travail. You will sense you have picked up someone's burden. If you begin praying with your mind, you may know whom you are praying for; then if you shift into praying in the Spirit, you may start agonizing (as in the childbirth-like labor we discussed earlier) over this person or situation with only prayers in the Spirit. As your prayers ascend to heaven, you can have faith to believe they will come down in blessings. As our prayers arise to the Lord as incense, we can believe the angels will take those prayers and fire from the altars of heaven and release them upon Earth. Goll says, "Intercession releases God's brilliant light or lightning to 'strike the mark' in the earth, directing God's power and glory into desired situations with supernatural results."[18]

In Isaiah 59:16, God laments—"And He saw that there was no man, And was astonished that there was no one to intercede; Then His own arm brought salvation to Him, And His righteousness upheld Him" (NASB). In the Hebrew, the word *intercede* used here is *paga*, which translates as "strikes the mark." "Intercession releases God's brilliant light or lightning to 'strike the mark' in the earth, directing God's power and glory into desired situations with supernatural results!...Intercession paints the target so God can zero in on areas of need with His glory!"[19]

Goll powerfully states the power of prayer and intercession thus: "Prayer works. Prayer is powerful. Prayer is one of our most deadly and effective weapons for destroying the works of the enemy. Prayer is God's lifeline to the hurting, the wounded, the weak, and the dying. But He expects you and I to throw out His rope of life in the name of His Son, Jesus. Intercession isn't the preoccupation of the zealous few—it is the calling and destiny of the Chosen people, of every blood-washed child of God. If you call Jesus Christ Savior and Lord, then He calls you intercessor and priest, and today He is calling you to your knees."[20]

Think About It

1. Why is praying in the Spirit (tongues) important? List the many reasons.
2. Explain why praying in tongues is a gateway into the supernatural realm of the Spirit.
3. Why do you think some churches disregard praying in the Spirit (tongues) as strange or unusual or even wrong rather than seek God's revelation about what the Word has to say about it?
4. What is the difference between the gift of tongues and praying in the Spirit?

Chapter 6

GIFTS OF THE HOLY SPIRIT

"If you have been baptized in the Holy Spirit," Dennis and Rita Bennett write, "you are probably becoming more aware of the gifts of the Spirit. Two words are used commonly in speaking of the gifts: one is *charisma* (or plural, *charismata*), gift of God's love; the other is *phanerosis,* manifestation."[21]

The word *gift* used in this context reminds us that these blessings come from God, freely given to His children. The word *manifestation* suggests a "showing forth, a making visible, or making known."[22] The Holy Spirit makes known His gifts through His children as the gifts come forth for the strengthening of the church. The gifts are not *ours* but belong to the person who receives the blessing from the ministry through the gift.

"The body of Christ is made up of many members, and God has purposely planned the release of the gifts 'as He wills' so that Christians would need one another in order to function effectively for Him."[23] The gifts of the Spirit are ways God releases His power in the life of a believer. The fruit of the Spirit is the character of Jesus being revealed in the life of a believer. Both the gifts and the fruit are important in furthering the kingdom of God. As Paul stated in 1 Corinthians 12:1, "Now concerning spiritual gifts, brethren, I do not want you to be ignorant" (NKJV).

It is important to remember that just because a person manifests the gifts of the Spirit does not mean he is walking closely with the Lord. Be careful to not "follow" a person just because he moves in the gifts of the Spirit. Look for fruit in his life, as well as honesty and truth and a knowledge and appreciation of God's Word. As you mature in your faith, look for balanced teaching as you "study to show yourself approved," and receive only what is quickened in your spirit by the Holy Spirit. "Remember Christians don't follow signs, signs follow Christians."[24]

Romans 12:6 suggests that gifts are manifested according to your faith. All we have to do to "move" in the gifts of the Holy Spirit is to make ourselves available to be a vessel through which the Spirit can flow. Our lack of faith limits God's ability to use us. As we yield to the Spirit and move in faith we open ourselves to the power of the Holy Spirit. It is not only by faith the gifts of the Spirit operate, but also to the degree you yield yourself to the Spirit.[25] Ask the Lord to start developing the gifts of the Spirit in your life. The more you yield to Him, the more spiritual gifts will become evident in your life.

In his book *A Discipleship Journey: A Navigational Guide to Spiritual Formation and Mentoring,* Dave Buehring provides insight into spiritual gifts.[26] You might also find information of interest in *Flowing in the Holy Ghost: A Practical Handbook on the Gifts of the Spirit* by Rodney M. Howard-Browne.[27] A third book—written during the 1970s when God was pouring out His Spirit across the body of Christ in many denominations—Dennis and Rita Bennett's *The Holy Spirit and You,* brings truth and simplicity to understanding the outworking of the gifts of the Spirit.[28] I have drawn primarily upon these three books in my discussion of the outworking of the gifts of the Holy Spirit.

> Now about the spiritual gifts (the special endowments of supernatural energy), brethren, I do not want you to be misinformed. You know that when you were heathen, you were led off after idols that could not speak [habitually] as impulse directed and whenever the occasion might arise. Therefore I want you to understand that

> no one speaking under the power and influence of the [Holy] Spirit of God can [ever] say, Jesus be cursed! And no one can [really] say, Jesus is [my] Lord, except by and under the power and influence of the Holy Spirit. Now there are distinctive varieties and distributions of endowments (gifts, extraordinary powers distinguishing certain Christians, due to the power of divine grace operating in their souls by the Holy Spirit) and they vary, but the [Holy] Spirit remains the same. And there are distinctive varieties of service and ministration, but it is the same Lord [Who is served]. And there are distinctive varieties of operation [of working to accomplish things], but it is the same God Who inspires and energizes them all in all. But to each one is given the manifestation of the [Holy] Spirit [the evidence, the spiritual illumination of the Spirit] for good and profit. To one is given in and through the [Holy] Spirit [the power to speak] a message of wisdom, and to another [the power to express] a word of knowledge and understanding according to the same [Holy] Spirit; To another [wonder-working] faith by the same [Holy] Spirit, to another the extraordinary powers of healing by the one Spirit; To another the working of miracles, to another prophetic insight (the gift of interpreting the divine will and purpose); to another the ability to discern and distinguish between [the utterances of true] spirits [and false ones], to another various kinds of [unknown] tongues, to another the ability to interpret [such] tongues.
>
> —1 Corinthians 12:1–10, amp

It is important to understand that the nine gifts of the Holy Spirit are all supernatural. The gifts are given and imparted to you by the Spirit; you become a vessel from which they flow. You have the choice of welcoming the gifts and allowing them to flow freely, or staying closed to the supernatural realm of God. Ownership of the gift or gifts belongs to God. He allows us to participate in His purposes by pouring out His Spirit through His presence, His glory, and His gifts.

The spiritual gifts listed in 1 Corinthians 12:1–10 are:

- Word of wisdom
- Word of knowledge
- Faith
- Gifts of healing
- Working of miracles
- Prophecy
- Distinguishing between spirits (discernment of spirits)
- Speaking in different tongues (divers kinds of tongues, 1 Cor. 12:10, KJV)
- Interpretation of tongues

In 1 Corinthians 14:13–15 Paul says, "For this reason anyone who speaks in a tongue should pray that he may interpret what he says. For if I pray in a tongue, my spirit prays, but my mind is unfruitful…I will sing with my spirit, but I will also sing with my mind." Verses 18 and 19 continue, "I thank God that I speak in tongues more than all of you. But in the church I would rather speak five intelligible words to instruct others than ten thousand words in a tongue."

Revelation Gifts (The Power to Know)

The gifts of revelation are: word of wisdom, word of knowledge, and discerning of spirits. The revelation gifts consist of information supernaturally revealed by God. The Bennetts say that "each of these gifts is the God-given ability to receive from Him facts concerning something, anything, about which it is humanly impossible for us to know, revealed to the believer so that he may be protected, pray more effectively, or help someone in need."[29]

Word of wisdom and word of knowledge

A word of wisdom and a word of knowledge may work in conjunction to bring forth God's plan and purposes. A word of wisdom is supernatural wisdom given by the Holy Spirit to further God's purposes in a given situation. Buehring tells us, "Wisdom is the supernatural ability given by God to receive impressions of wisdom, which otherwise may not have been known, to apply to a person or situation for God's purposes."[30] The Bennetts note it is the "supernatural application of knowledge" that gives you proper judgment for action.[31] The supernatural gift of wisdom may provide solutions in the midst of conflict and confusion. A word of wisdom is a God-solution, or godly insight, into circumstances or situations. When a person is sensitive to the Holy Spirit's direction, he may receive insight from God that can be infused into a situation to bring an immediate answer to a complex issue. You will sense the presence of the Holy Spirit and know that this wisdom was from above and not your wisdom. The gift of wisdom and the gift of knowledge often work in tandem. The word of wisdom will instruct you as to how to solve problems, speak into complex situations, and find solutions for difficult challenges.

The Holy Spirit gives knowledge or impressions that are supernatural and impossible for you to know on your own. These promptings or impressions may come in a variety of ways, including seeing with the mind's eye, feeling physical pain, an inner knowing, inner pictures or visions. When this information is acted upon, it releases God's power into the person or situation.

A word of wisdom or a word of knowledge may come through a sudden thought or inspiration that lingers and does not leave you. It may be instruction or a solution or implementation of what you have heard from the Lord. These words may come as a strong "knowing" deep in your spirit, a vision, or the vocal gifts of the Spirit. These gifts are developed as you stay close to the Lord and seek Him continually. "The gifts of the Holy Spirit come from and through the Holy Spirit to our *spirit*, and not from or through the soul or physical senses."[32] If a Christian starts thinking of a person or becomes aware that a friend may be in trouble or needs prayer, this information comes from the Spirit. You may all of a sudden start thinking about a person and "see" or visualize him in a difficult or dangerous place and simply know he is in trouble. You may not know the specifics, but you know he needs prayer. A word of wisdom or word of knowledge can also come through dreams.

For example, in July of 1993 our church took forty youth to Hungary and Romania for a mission trip. We were stopped at the border of Romania, where the border guards refused to let us cross over because they wanted us to pay a significant bribe. While our translators discussed this situation with them, we were kept on the buses in one hundred-degree heat; we were told we'd be shot if we got off the buses. As the tension heightened and the temperature inside the un-air-conditioned buses rose, girls started fainting from heat exposure. One girl was in particularly bad shape and was removed from the bus. She was lying on a nearby rock being treated by Romanian nurses. Thousands of miles away in the States, in the middle of the night, a man had a vivid dream that his daughter was lying on a large rock, dying. He got up immediately, woke his wife, and together they began praying for their daughter. They had no idea that what he'd dreamed was, in fact, happening at that very moment. Eventually, so many teens were sick with heat stroke and dehydration that the border guards let us go. God heard the prayers of these parents and brought all of us to safety.

The following are some examples of the word of knowledge as given in the Bible. The prophet Nathan was given a word of knowledge about David's adulterous affair with Bathsheba. (See 2 Samuel 12:7–10.) Elisha knew the location of the Syrian army camp, which saved Israel from war. (See 2 Kings 6:8–23.) Time and again Elisha told the king the whereabouts of armies and kings coming against Israel. Jesus moved in a word of knowledge when he "saw" Nathanael under the fig tree and said to him, "Here is a true Israelite, in whom there is nothing false" (John 1:47). When Jesus saw the woman at the well in Samaria, He spoke to her through a word of knowledge, telling her about her many husbands. She was so amazed about Him knowing so much about her, she ran back to the town to tell what Jesus said to her. (See John 4:9–31.) Throughout Jesus' life, He operated in all realms of the supernatural, but especially in the word of knowledge and wisdom. By a word of knowledge, the Spirit revealed to Peter that three men were in Joppa at the gate looking for him. So, when the men arrived, Peter went with them to Cornelius's house, knowing that the Lord had arranged the meeting. (See Acts 10:17–23.) The Spirit revealed to Peter that Ananias and Sapphira kept back part of the money from a piece of property they sold; because they lied to the Holy Spirit, when Peter spoke, they both fell down and died. (See Acts 5:1–10.) There are countless examples in the Old and New Testaments of men of God speaking with the supernatural power of the word of wisdom and knowledge.

Examples of a word of wisdom in the Old Testament include stories such as the time Joseph interpreted Pharaoh's dream with supernatural knowledge and wisdom to provide the solution to the famine problem. (See Genesis 41.) God gave Daniel great natural wisdom and knowledge, but also gave him a supernatural word of knowledge when he interpreted King Nebuchadnezzar's dream. (See Daniel 2.) He was also called upon to interpret the handwriting on the wall for King Belshazzar. Another example may be found in Acts 15:13–21, when James brought supernatural wisdom to the Jerusalem Council. James's wisdom addressed how Gentiles could turn to God without becoming Jews. His wisdom was straightforward and simple and was well received by the apostles and elders of the church.

Discerning of spirits

As Christians grow in faith, their minds and consciences should reflect the mind of Christ. As they mature, when something is of the Holy Spirit, they should have spiritual receptors that recognize the presence and move of the Spirit. They should also be able to bear witness (that internal knowing) that something is amiss and not of the Spirit. Christians may have the gift of discerning of spirits, but it becomes intensified after the baptism of the Holy Spirit.

Rodney Howard-Browne explains:

> The supernatural gift of discerning spirits is a divine ability to see and discern in three areas:
>
> 1. When the Holy Spirit is moving
> 2. The presence of demons or angels
> 3. False doctrine, false prophets; and looking into the hearts of men—(lies)[33]

The discerning of spirits allows you to see (discern) when and how the Holy Spirit is moving. You know this by the Spirit of God. “The gift of discerning of spirits operates in the area of demons, angels, or natural human spirits.”[34] When this gift is in operation, you will be able to see or discern when angels or demons are present. You will also be able to determine what is in the hearts of people and their motivation. When something is not from God or wrong in a situation or a person, you will have a “check” in your spirit. An example of this gift in operation occurs in Acts 5:1–10, when Peter confronted Ananias and Sapphira, as mentioned above.

This gift enables believers to know what is motivating a person or situation. A person might be expressing his own thoughts or feelings, or be operating in the inspiration of the Holy Spirit. Or demonic spirits may be oppressing a person or situation. The gift of discerning of spirits uncovers what is taking place. The presence of the Holy Spirit brings peace. Demonic spirits bring unrest, heaviness, or a restless spirit.

Spiritual discernment lets you know when something is wrong. We were in the middle of a prayer group at my house, and a friend from the past came in the front door. She didn't speak but walked aggressively into the prayer group. I could sense when she walked through the door that something was not right, but I didn't know what. As she moved into the circle of people, there was an inappropriate aggressiveness toward some of the members of the group. Before long, her presence had disrupted the entire group. As the leader of the group, I was caught off guard, because I had never had someone join our group and behave that way. I should have stopped the group and asked the Holy Spirit to reveal the cause of the problem. I should have also addressed her improper behavior in a proper way.

Sometimes people can say the right thing, but they are moving in the wrong spirit. Part of what they say and do may be right on, but something doesn't line up in your spirit. A spirit of divination, manipulation, or rebellion, or other such disturbance, might have been sent by the devil to bring a counterfeit message.

Discerning of spirits also operates as a warning signal so you will be able to discern false doctrine, false prophets, and false prophecies. It also gives you the ability to supernaturally know when someone is lying to you. Christians young in the Lord will not usually be able to discern these things in the Holy Spirit, because these revelations usually come to people who are more spiritually mature and who hear the voice of the Lord.

"All of the revelation gifts reveal something: *knowledge.* The word of knowledge is knowledge. The word of wisdom is knowledge. The discerning of spirits is knowledge. You know something through the operation of these gifts."[35] There is often overlap in the gifts of revelation. The word of knowledge will come forth in conjunction with a word of wisdom, which may be linked to discerning of spirits. Sometimes the manifestation of each will be so clear you will be able to easily understand which one is in operation; at other times you may not be able to tell.[36]

There are many examples of discerning of spirits in the Scriptures. In Acts 16, a woman spoke these words, "These men are the servants of the most High God, who proclaim to you the way of salvation" (v. 17, ESV), but she was speaking under the influence of an unclean spirit. Paul discerned the evil spirit in the woman, commanded it to leave, and the woman was set free.

The gift of discerning of spirits is also used in conjunction with bringing relief to a person bound by the enemy through an evil spirit. Jesus was constantly casting out demons, which made up a big portion of His ministry. He further said that believers would cast out demons in His name. The Scriptures state, "Submit yourself, then, to God. Resist the devil, and he will flee from you" (James 4:7). It is important to understand and walk in the full authority that has been given to you as a child of God. In Mark 16:17, the Word says, "In my name they will drive out demons."

The question is often asked, Can a Christian be possessed by a spirit? The Bennetts say, "A Christian cannot be possessed in his spirit (where the Holy Spirit dwells), but his mind, emotions or will (the three parts of his soul) may be depressed, oppressed, obsessed, or even possessed if he has let the enemy in by choosing to live in known sin rather than with the Lord Jesus. A non-Christian, of course, may be possessed, spirit, soul, and body."[37]

For you to grow in the revelation gifts, you must spend time alone with the Lord. Seeking His presence and learning to become sensitive to the Holy Spirit will allow you to grow and become sensitive to the anointing. As you spend time with him, you will start to learn the ways of the Spirit. Learning to hear His voice happens as you spend time alone with Him in communion. You will be able to discern His voice and the voice of your own spirit. As you grow in your knowledge of the Lord and seek to grow in His ways, ask Him for the gifts of the Spirit to be evident in your life.

Power Gifts (The Power to Do)

The power gifts include the gifts of faith, healing, and miracles. These gifts are the extension of the compassion of Jesus to a hurting world. He spent His ministry loving, caring for, and healing the sick, dying, and perishing. He says in John 14:12, "He who believes in Me, the works that I do, he will do also; and greater works than these he will do; because I go to the Father" (NASB). His desire is for His children to live in the Spirit and His power, doing the works He did while on Earth.

Gift of faith

"Now faith is being sure of what we hope for and certain of what we do not see" (Heb. 11:1). This means that faith is active and in the now! In Acts 16:31 the Scriptures say, "Believe in the Lord Jesus, and you will be saved." This kind of faith—saving faith—is a gift from God, which comes from being drawn nigh to God by the Holy Spirit. All believers have access to the gift of faith, but as is the case with all the gifts of the Spirit, after the baptism of the Holy Spirit, the gift of faith becomes truly active.

The gift of faith is one of the power gifts—God's power to release miracles! Supernatural faith is the ability to believe in a supernatural miracle, having absolute, unwavering faith that God is going to do something powerful. Pentecostal evangelist Smith Wigglesworth lived and moved in the word of faith so supernaturally that he commanded the dead to come back to life on several occasions, and people came back to life just like the day that Jesus commanded Lazarus to come out of the tomb. A word of faith makes onlookers nervous because they are observing the raw power of God. People with the gift of faith have immovable faith to believe God for the impossible when others around them don't. These people "see" things as already done, and God intervenes supernaturally on their behalf. Browne says, "The gift of faith is a divine supernatural manifestation of God's faith imparted to you at a specific time, at a specific place, for a specific purpose."[38] God pours His faith into you, and you start to experience the supernatural until the gift lifts. Then you wonder what just happened.

When you are moving in the gift of faith, Holy Spirit boldness comes upon you and you say and do things that are contrary to the natural man (as opposed to the spiritual man or woman). Supernatural faith was evident in the life of Elijah when he confronted King Ahab and the prophets of Ba'al on Mt. Carmel. Daniel lived in supernatural faith when he was thrown in the lion's den and God spared his life. The disciples ministered in the supernatural gift of faith as people were healed, delivered, and set free. An example of the gift of faith is seen in Acts 3:1–6 when Peter and John healed the lame man at the temple. Miracles are still taking place as believers lay hands on the sick or the dead. There are countless reports of people being raised from the dead around the world as Christians lay hands on them and release the power of Jesus' name through the gift of faith.

Gift of healing

The gift of healing is a supernatural ability given by the Holy Spirit to restore health and wholeness to a person without natural means. Healing is the eradication of sickness or disease. God leads and directs us to those in need for whom we pray, but He is the healer. He just uses us as a vessel—we are His coworkers. Any believer can pray for the sick and see them healed in the name of Jesus. However, after the baptism of the Holy Spirit, faith increases for the gift of healing, and the person starts to minister to the sick. As with all gifts of the Spirit, after the baptism of the Spirit all gifts intensify and come forth based on a person's level of faith and hunger to see the gifts manifest. The more a person desires spiritual gifts to be active in his life, the more these gifts will become evident. Various types of healings include physical, emotional, and spiritual healing. People with this gift operate out of compassion and desire to see others get well. They sense God's presence to heal, and they are sensitive to the Spirit's power for healing.

Healing can come from prayer, touch, words spoken, or prophetic words. Jesus' miracles of healing appear all through the Gospels. Healings can be instantaneous or gradual over time.

Jesus healed the sick in a variety of ways. Sometimes He spoke. Other times He commanded, and in many other ways healing was released into desperate lives. Sometimes He laid hands on the sick. In James 5:14–15, "Is any one of you sick? He should call the elders of the church to pray over him and anoint him with oil in the name of the Lord. And the prayer offered in faith will make the sick person well; the Lord will raise him up." If we practiced this scriptural path to healing, it would be interesting to see how many people would be healed.

Bennett says we have no scriptural basis to end a prayer with "the faith-destroying phrase, 'If it be Thy will!' God has made perfectly clear in His word that it is His will to heal the sick."[39] The Bible tells us repeatedly that God desires to heal the sick. "I am the LORD, who heals you," we learn in Exodus 15:26. In Psalm 103:2–3 we learn, "Praise the LORD, O my soul, and forget not all his benefits—who forgives all your sins and heals all your diseases."

Along with the gift of healing, the gift of wisdom or knowledge may also be in operation. Maybe the gift of faith is also present. Faith is necessary for a healing ministry. Repentance and confession are sometimes necessary before healing if the recipient has unrepentant sin, bitterness, and resentment. Sometimes sin and a root of bitterness and unforgiveness open the door for the spirit of infirmity to take hold of our lives, resulting in sickness and disease.

Rodney Howard-Browne says, "Some people don't need healing; they need a miracle. If half of a man's stomach is eaten away with cancer, he doesn't need a healing; he's not sick. Half his stomach is gone. He needs a miracle! If he had a miracle, he wouldn't have a problem."[40] While Jesus was on Earth, He healed the sick and destroyed the works of the devil, but nowadays we wonder why we don't see more miracles and supernatural healings. One reason may be because we don't expect to see the Holy Spirit do anything supernatural. If you are interested in allowing God to give you the gift of healing, then ask Him for this supernatural gift. The best way to gain knowledge of this gift is to start praying for the sick.

Working of miracles

The working of miracles is a power gift that the Holy Spirit releases when the situation calls for miracles. Miracles seem to override the so-called laws of nature, and they bring great glory to God. Often the working of miracles is released to authenticate the gospel of Christ with signs and wonders that point to Jesus as Lord and Savior. This power may include deliverance from demonic strongholds.

The apostles worked miracles by the power of the Holy Spirit, and thus was God's kingdom established on Earth. Thousands came into the kingdom because of the supernatural power that was released through miracles and healings. Jesus said that when He ascended, we would do greater things than He did, and it appears that this may come to pass. People are being transported physically in the Spirit, as Philip the evangelist was in Acts 8:39–40. In the past few decades, powerful revivals have broken out in Indonesia, China, South Korea, and other nations of the world. There are reports in magazines, documentaries, and books about the supernatural power of the Holy Spirit being released around the world. People are being supernaturally fed, walking on water, being healed with creative miracles (including blind eyes seeing, limbs growing, the paralyzed walking), and people are raised from the dead in the powerful name of Jesus.

You may have to pray for a lot of people before God releases the gift of miracles, but one day as you are faithfully serving and believing the Lord, the supernatural gift of the working of miracles may fall on you in an instant, and you will be able to watch God work powerful miracles through you. You must learn to contend and fight for the supernatural power of God to be made manifest in your life. Be willing to believe for the supernatural, pray for the supernatural, and experience the supernatural. God did not intend for His children to be bored with the Christian experience. He died for our salvation, freedom, and to empower us with the Spirit and the gifts for the advancing of His kingdom. Shake off everything that holds you bound to tradition and break free as the Holy Spirit takes you into higher realms of His glory.

Inspirational Gifts—Gifts of Utterance (The Power to Say)

The inspirational gifts include what we might speak to a fallen world: the gifts of prophecy, of speaking in tongues, and interpretation of the speaking in tongues.

> Follow the way of love and eagerly desire spiritual gifts, especially the gift of prophecy. For anyone who speaks in a tongue does not speak to men but to God. Indeed, no one understands him; he utters mysteries with his spirit. But everyone who prophesies speaks to men for their strengthening, encouragement and comfort. He who speaks in a tongue edifies himself, but he who prophesies edifies the church. I would like every one of you to speak in tongues, but I would rather have you prophesy. He who prophesies is greater than one who speaks in tongues, unless he interprets, so that the church may be edified. Now, brothers, if I come to you and speak in tongues, what good will I be to you, unless I bring you some revelation or knowledge or prophecy or word of instruction?
>
> —1 Corinthians 14:1–6

> For this reason anyone who speaks in a tongue should pray that he may interpret what he says. For if I pray in a tongue, my spirit prays, but my mind is unfruitful.

> So what shall I do? I will pray with my spirit, but I will also pray with my mind; I will sing with my spirit, but I will also sing with my mind. If you are praising God with your spirit, how can one who finds himself among those who do not understand say "Amen" to your thanksgiving, since he does not know what you are saying? You may be giving thanks well enough, but the other man is not edified
>
> —1 Corinthians 14:13–17

Prophecy

Believers speak the mind of God through the gift of prophecy. Prophecy comes forth in a known language, and believers and unbelievers are able to understand the word. In 1 Corinthians 14:39, Paul says, "Therefore, my brothers, be eager to prophesy, and do not forbid speaking in tongues." Prophecy is for the edification of believers and, secondly, for unbelievers. Prophecy ministers to believers by edification, exhortation, comfort, and strengthening. (See 1 Corinthians 14:3.) The Scriptures also say, "But if an unbeliever or someone who does not understand comes in while everybody is prophesying, he will be convinced by all that he is a sinner and will be judged by all, and the secrets of his heart will be laid bare. So he will fall down and worship God, exclaiming, 'God is really among you!'" (1 Cor. 14:24–25).

"The gifts of utterance—tongues, interpretation, and prophecy—are not to guide our lives by," the Bennetts tell us, "but to help unfold God to us, and to help us in our response to Him. They are to turn us God-ward and to give us a healthy fear (awe) of the Lord."[41] And Scripture reiterates, "But everyone who prophesies speaks to men for their strengthening, encouragement and comfort" (1 Cor. 14:3), and "He who prophesies edifies the church" (1 Cor. 14:4). Prophesying is a God-inspired utterance using a known language. Prophecies are given by the Holy Spirit, and they flow forth and spring out of your innermost being. Prophecy can give direction and guidance, encouragement and confidence to move forward to do God's will in your life. The supernatural gift of prophecy in the New Testament was given to Christians for edifying the church but also for the release of the Word of God into a particular situation. Prophecy can foretell, make known one's thoughts, or illuminate something the Holy Spirit is trying to make known. Prophecy is the supernatural ability of the Holy Spirit to proclaim truth for the purpose of strengthening the church. A person who moves in the prophetic gift is able to quickly discern the motives, intentions, and attitudes of others. He is dependent on the Scriptures to validate his words and is bold and willing to speak up and speak out the words, or messages, he receives from the Lord. These prophetic, supernatural words often result in conviction, repentance, redirection, or realignment with God's purposes for your life.

First Corinthians 14 explains the outworking of the gift of prophecy within the church. In summary, this scripture says that prophecy is for unbelievers. If an unbeliever or someone who does not understand what is going on comes in while someone is prophesying, the non-Christian will be convinced by what he experiences and "the secrets of his heart will be laid bare" (1 Cor. 14:25). There are many excellent books written on the gift of prophecy. The scope of this writing is simply to introduce you to spiritual gifts and stir up hunger so you will seek God for the gifts of the Holy Spirit and the outworking of those gifts.

Prophets of the Old Testament were often moved by God to prophesy. They ministered through the gift of prophecy and knowledge and often did mighty miracles by the power of the Holy Spirit. On the day of Pentecost, Peter quoted the words of Joel:

> In the last days, God says, I will pour out my Spirit on all people. Your sons and daughters will prophesy, your young men will see visions, your old men will dream dreams. Even on my servants, both men and women,

> I will pour out my Spirit in those days, and they will prophesy.
>
> —Acts 2:17–18

Prophecy is to be a part of every believer's life. The Word says in 1 Corinthians 14:39, "Desire earnestly to prophesy, and do not forbid to speak in tongues" (NASB). Paul stated that he wished that all prophesied. This is a gift the Holy Spirit gives to those who ask. Prophecy is for the community of God. Prophecy is to be delivered publically so that it can be evaluated and judged by the church. If the prophet is of God, there will be a witness of the Spirit in the hearts of the believers, and the word will be in agreement with the written Word of God.

There are different levels of the prophetic, and a difference between the gift of prophecy and the office of the prophet. The office of a prophet is held by those who by the Spirit prophesy concerning such matters as times, places, and events—usually with great precision. The office of the prophet often links up with other supernatural gifts, such as the word of wisdom and the word of knowledge. Some prophets freely move in the power gifts. Agabus, in the New Testament, is an example of someone who probably served God in the office of prophet. Samuel, Elijah, Elisha, and Isaiah are examples of Old Testament prophets. Today we have prophets who hold the office of prophet. There are people alive today who are recognized internationally by the body of Christ as prophets: Chuck Pierce, James Goll, Cindy Jacobs, Patricia King, and many others.

The ministry of the apostle has not come to an end, and the apostolic age is still in operation throughout the church. The body of Christ needs both the office of apostle and prophet to be scripturally equipped. Ephesians 4:11–13 states, "It was he who gave some to be apostles, some to be prophets, some to be evangelists, and some to be pastors and teachers, to prepare God's people for works of service, so that the body of Christ may be built up until we all reach unity in the faith and in the knowledge of the Son of God and become mature, attaining to the whole measure of the fullness of Christ." Real prophets do not have to make announcements that they are prophets because they will be recognized by their ministry. They declare both the will and mind of God by His Spirit. Apostles and prophets did not disappear when the first apostles died, although many denominations teach this. Would it make any sense for God to say in His Word that apostles and prophets are needed for the building up of the body of Christ, but then not appoint and anoint apostles and prophets from the birth of the church forward? Our religious and spiritual paradigm needs to open up and shift to see the amazing things God is doing in the world through His prophets and apostles. Ask God to start revealing truth to you and to open your eyes to the amazing things He is doing in the Spirit and in the body of Christ.

A person who is in the office of a prophet will be a mature Christian. His doctrine and manner of life should be known to the Christian community to whom he prophesies. True prophets will lift up Jesus and draw men to God, not to themselves. A prophet's words must also line up with the Word and be tested by the Spirit. First Corinthians 13:9 says, "We prophesy in part," meaning the Holy Spirit imparts as much or as little as He feels need for.

There are plenty of false prophets in the world, and the devil counterfeits all true gifts. People who start religious sects and use their power to wrongly influence others will keep their people in bondage by fear. They will separate adherents from their families and the body of Christ. There are many such sects who call themselves by the name of Jesus when, in fact, Paul says, "Savage wolves will come in among you and will not spare the flock" (Acts 20:29). If you find yourself in the kind of group that wants to monitor everything you do, read, and who you fellowship with, you need to get yourself out of this insidious web of deception. As a psychologist, I have seen clients who have been caught in the death trap of cultish groups that pretend to be a part of the body of Christ but are, in fact, caught in the deception and manipulation of someone who wants power at the cost of the people he or she is supposed to serve. Cultist leaders pull you away from your family. Take heed and be warned. All things must be judged. If you sense something is just not right, then pay attention to the lack of peace you have by the direction of the Holy Spirit.

When a word of personal prophecy is given, it needs to be given by a mature and submitted man or woman of God. There needs to be a witness of the Spirit on the part of the person receiving the word. Never do something just because a friend comes to you and says, "Thus saith the Lord!" You have a personal responsibility to pray over the word, wait on the Lord, and take the word to other believers who walk closely with you to discern the accuracy of the word over your life.

A few months ago in a prayer group, a woman who seldom attended the group started prophesying and declaring words over me that I did not bear witness with. I stopped her in mid-stream and said, "Stop. I don't bear witness to what you are saying." My spirit was about to jump out of my body, so I knew at many levels she had missed the mark. I then started rebuking the word, saying, "In the name of Jesus I break the power of this word over my life. I reject in the name of Jesus what has been spoken over my life." I then demanded she stop speaking over me. I believe if I had not stopped and rejected what she had spoken, it would have undone all the breakthroughs God had brought forth for me in the previous months and would have set me on a course of destruction.

The gift of prophecy can be a powerful word from the Lord, but it is up to all of us to weigh those words by the Word of God, the inner witness of our spirit and the Spirit, and receive godly counsel from others.

Speaking in different tongues and interpretation

Tongues and interpretation should always be manifested together in a public meeting. Some have suggested that speaking in tongues and interpretation of tongues are the least of the gifts, because they are listed last in 1 Corinthians 12:7–11. The Bennetts conclude that these gifts were given to the church last because the first seven gifts (wisdom, knowledge, faith, healings, miracles, prophecy, and discerning of spirits) "are found in the Old Testament and the Gospels, but these two gifts were not given until Pentecost."[42]

Speaking in tongues can be manifested in two ways. The most common is in the prayer language/devotional language for private edification, which needs no interpretation. However, as you pray in the Spirit, the Lord may give you an interpretation as you journal your "letter from the Lord." While praying in the Spirit, you may receive a strong impression from the Lord. If in faith you start to write what you are sensing or "hearing," you may discover the Lord is speaking to you through your prayer language. The second, public manifestation of tongues will be referred to as the gift of tongues. The gift of tongues is delivered to the listeners, and they are encouraged and blessed by the interpretation that follows. In 1 Corinthians 14:13–15 Paul says, "For this reason anyone who speaks in a tongue should pray that he may interpret what he says, For if I pray in a tongue, my spirit prays, but my mind is unfruitful…I will sing with my spirit, but I will also sing with my mind." Verses 18–19 continue, "I thank God that I speak in tongues more than all of you. But in the church I would rather speak five intelligible words to instruct others than ten thousand words in a tongue."

To eliminate confusion, tongues and interpretation should be released in groups of believers who have been instructed about the gifts and understand their significance. Speaking in tongues is one of the nine gifts of the Holy Spirit, and these words are spoken as the Spirit wills. Your prayer language is under your control, because you can pray in the Spirit whenever you want to, but you are not able to give a *message* in tongues when you want to. Messages in tongues are powerful and anointed, and there will always be an interpretation. You should never deliver a tongue unless you are spiritually equipped to give the interpretation. Again, speaking in tongues is a sign to unbelievers: "Divers tongues plus the interpretation of tongues is the equivalent of prophetic utterance."[43] Divers tongues speak directly to a person or persons or the entire church body when delivered under the anointing. Lives are changed, people are healed, and the kingdom of God advances. Now is the time for the body of Christ to receive the baptism in the Spirit and start allowing God to give us the gifts of the Spirit. It is important the church no longer takes lightly prophecy, divers tongues, and interpretation.

When you are praying in your prayer language (unknown tongue), you are speaking mysteries unto God. (See 1 Corinthians 14:2.) You don't know what you are praying, but you are praying the perfect will of God. It is important that you exercise your prayer language and pray in tongues often. By doing so you are stirring up the Spirit within. As you grow and mature, it is important to move into the higher and deeper realms of the Spirit. Seek His face, and spiritual anointing will increase. Jude 20 says to "build yourselves up in your most holy faith and pray in the Holy Spirit."

YIELDING TO THE HOLY SPIRIT

When the Holy Spirit comes upon you, He is usually prompting you to do or say something. Once baptized in the Spirit, you will feel a stirring within your spirit when the anointing is on you for a specific reason. If you are not willing to yield and move in the things of the Spirit, He will stop prompting and will leave you alone. If He speaks to you time and time again and you refuse to yield to what He is asking you to do, He will stop coming to you. This is what it means to *quench the Spirit*.

The anointing comes in various forms. Sometimes your heart starts to pound. Sometimes your hands start to tingle and perspire.

Sometimes you feel like you have been bathed in hot water or oil. Under intense anointing, you can feel like your body is on fire. You may feel the "fire" of God on you and your heart pounding and you may have the "word" of the Lord. These are physical manifestations that confirm the Holy Spirit is "on you." In faith, you need to stand up and speak forth or do whatever God has called you to do; however, wait for the proper timing. You will instinctively know when the Spirit wants you to deliver the word. The Lord will often give you the same word more than one time until it is time to deliver the word.

Sometimes the Holy Spirit Moves Away from Churches

One of the reasons traditional religion disregards the baptism of the Holy Spirit and the gifts of the Spirit is because the Holy Spirit cannot be controlled or manipulated. I attended a nondenominational church during the outpouring of the Holy Spirit in the late 1960s and early 1970s. Many of the members were receiving the baptism of the Holy Spirit and experiencing newfound joy, excitement, and supernatural encounters with Jesus. Spiritual gifts were beginning to flow in the church services (i.e., words of prophecy, gift of tongues, with the gift of interpretation). Because allowing the Holy Spirit to flow in the church service took away control from church leaders, after a while people were asked to not engage in these gifts while at church. Some church leaders often prefer a predictable service rather than a service where the Holy Spirit and His gifts are welcome. This church made a decision that they approved of members exercising and experiencing dimensions of the Holy Spirit outside of church (in home groups and other gatherings, for example) but not in the church services. The bottom line was church leaders were not comfortable with providing the Holy Spirit freedom to have His way in church services. They were more concerned about offending members than they were about offending the Holy Spirit. The result was a church service with great freedom of worship yet restraint on the Holy Spirit for fear He might do something unpredictable. What I have discovered in the past thirty-five years is that most Christians and churches are more concerned about offending their fellow man than they are about offending the Holy Spirit. No wonder the supernatural power of the most high God does not flow through our churches! No wonder we are deprived of the creative miracles, divine healings, powerful life transformations, and revival that could bring reform to our nation!

Without power from the Holy Spirit and without welcoming Him to come and invade our lives, families, churches, and nation, we hold back the very power of God from coming to dwell among us. We need to get beyond being so concerned about what others think and become more concerned about what the Holy Spirit thinks. The fear of man robs us of freedom to worship. Most Christians stand before God in a frozen state during worship, afraid to raise their arms to praise, clap, shout, or do anything that shows exuberance for God. They think, "We have never done it that way before," or "What will my friends think?" Who cares what your friends think! It is time to arise and praise our God with all of our might, power, and strength!

Several years ago, in 1992, the Holy Spirit spoke to me in a large church and told me to dance before Him. It was a large charismatic church, but it was before the days of people dancing before the Lord in church. I could not believe my ears, so I said, "Lord, are you telling me to dance before You right now?" He clearly said, "Yes!" I was dressed in a beautiful suit, heels, and had come to church feeling sophisticated; yet, the Lord clearly was not concerned about any of these superficial things, but rather He was interested in my obedience. Many years before, when I had received the baptism of the Holy Spirit, I had made a commitment to the Lord that I would be more concerned about offending Him and less concerned about offending others. So I stepped out into the aisle, and I danced before the Lord with all my heart. That day I broke through to a new spiritual level.

I had another powerful experience at church during a Saturday night service. At the time I attended a large charismatic church in Nashville, and by this time it *was* customary to see people dancing and worshiping the Lord in the aisles. This particular night I was dead tired from working in the yard all day and could barely walk due to a hip injury I had about a year earlier. As worship started, I heard the Spirit say, "Dance!" Being a psychologist, I had several clients who were in this particular service, a lawyer in particular, and to be honest I was embarrassed to dance before the Lord. He spoke again, "Dance!" The second time it was undeniable that the Lord was asking me to humble myself before Him and to be obedient. When I said, "Yes, Lord!" He then said, "When you dance, I will heal your hip." After dancing before Him that night and not caring what others thought about it, He healed my hip. God is looking for people who will learn to discern His voice, be obedient, and follow Him wherever He leads.

It is astounding to me when I attend church services with glorious worship and yet church members stand in the midst of God's glory frozen—standing there stiff as a board. Few raise holy hands before the Lord and freely worship the Lord. I believe the main reason is that people in general are far more concerned about embarrassing themselves and offending others than they are about worshiping the Lord. I believe it is time the body of Christ put aside denominational teaching and inhibitions and start inviting the Holy Spirit to come and invade their lives and churches. Too long, we have attended dead churches steeped in religion and the traditions of man and left the Holy Spirit out of our experience. It is long overdue for the church of Jesus Christ to arise in her power, clothed in the Holy Spirit and washed in the blood of the Lamb. Now is the time for revival to break out and Christians to be empowered with the Holy Spirit. It is time to move forth into the knowledge and experience of the baptism of the Holy Spirit and receive the gifts of the Spirit. It is time to praise our God by raising our hands and clapping and worshiping Him with all of our might in Spirit and in truth.

Think About It

1. How does praying in the Spirit open the door from prayer to intercession?
2. What are the benefits of praying in the Spirit (tongues)?
3. What is the difference between the gift of tongues and praying in the Spirit (tongues)?
4. When would a person speak forth a "tongue" in a public meeting? Why should the person need to have the faith and ability to interpret the word according to 1 Corinthians 14:13–15?
5. Why do you think Christians would be more afraid of offending others than offending the Holy Spirit?
6. Based on your answer to this question, how will your thinking, attitudes, and behavior change toward the Holy Spirit?
7. Are you more concerned about offending the Lord or offending others? Does the fear of man control your life? You cannot serve two masters.

Chapter 7

HEARING THE VOICE OF THE HOLY SPIRIT

TO GROW IN your faith, you need to be able to discern the voice of the Spirit as He guides and leads you. The Old Testament makes constant reference to the fact that Israel did not listen to God; thus, the nation wandered in rebellion and disobedience. God speaks powerfully by His Spirit, but His children need to learn to hear His voice and walk in His ways. In order to be in a relationship, there must be two-way communication, and we do that through prayer. God loves us and wants us to know Him.

God is still talking to His people, just like He did during biblical times. He spoke—and still speaks—by divine revelation, through dreams and visions. He spoke to prophets and angels and through His Holy Spirit. He still speaks in powerful, supernatural ways. The primary way God speaks to us today is through His Word. We have the divine revelation of God through the Bible; always go there first when seeking guidance and direction.

God also speaks to us today by His Spirit, who indwells us and leads us into all truth. The Spirit can use others to speak and give direction in our lives. Circumstances and situations can be used by the Holy Spirit to guide and lead us into God's purposes for our lives. God desires to communicate truth to us—truth about Himself, ourselves, and others. In order to discern the quiet voice of the Spirit and His ways in our lives, we must become aggressive listeners who come to Him, knocking and seeking for more of Him, looking for His truth and direction for our lives. As we seek Him more, we pray more; as we pray more, we listen more. As we seek and ask more, we begin to discern His ways in our lives.

A passive relationship with the Lord will not lead you into the deeper realm of the Spirit. You have to be willing to seek and experience more of the Spirit before you grow in discernment of His voice and His ways.

GOD GETS OUR ATTENTION

In Charles Stanley's 1985 book, *How to Listen to God*, he suggests that God gets our attention in several key ways, including through a restless spirit, a word from others, and disappointments.[44]

A restless spirit

The story of Esther is a good example. God gave King Ahasuerus a restless spirit; he could not sleep, so he got up and read the book of the records of daily events. (See Esther 6.) He discovered that Mordecai had actually saved his life, and this led to the Jews being set free from the king's edict of death.

God oftentimes causes us to become restless. Life may be going well, and out of nowhere we become dissatisfied and restless in our spirits. We can't explain it or even describe it, but there is a divine discomfort that comes over our lives. When we feel this way, we need to seek the Lord and ask what He is trying to say. He may be prompting you to move to another locale, change jobs or churches, or return to church. You may be in a dating relationship that He wants to end. He may want you to give up a leadership role or pick up a leadership role. Stop and listen to what the voice of the Spirit is saying.

A word from others

The Spirit often speaks through others. If we are in the Word daily, living in prayer, and seeking His Presence, then others may speak something to us that is a confirmation of what the Lord has already said to us personally.

I have the privilege of working with a friend who is a strong, spiritually mature intercessor. She is the administrator of my business. I will ponder, pray, and percolate something I think the Spirit is saying to me. Debbie will often come to our morning prayer times and say, "I think I heard the Lord say…" What she receives many times is the confirmation of the word or direction the Lord has already given to me.

In January 2009, in the middle of the economic downturn, I kept hearing the Spirit speaking to my spirit, "It is time to move into a professional office space." I had been seeing clients in a virtual office space, and Debbie had been doing the administrative work out of my home. Our business started growing, and we could no longer contain the business in two locations with limited office space. I sensed a move was pending but could not imagine how God could work out the details or the money for such a move. One Monday during our prayer time, she said she had heard the Lord say it was time for us to move out of the home and into professional office space—yet this was not a conversation we had had before. My spirit leapt within because it was the confirmation I had been waiting for. I called my realtor, and on Thursday we looked for office space; the first office we looked at had twelve-foot ceilings with handcrafted one-foot molding. The "library" had cherry bookshelves and a fireplace. It would eventually become my office. Within a week we had signed the contract and moved into the space three weeks later. As soon as we moved and got settled in, our business doubled, and we were working at full capacity. By praying faithfully for the business and for the wisdom to know what to do and when, we were sensitive to the Spirit and discerned His ways and heard His voice. We were able to be right on target when He was ready for us to move.

There are countless examples of God speaking to others on our behalf in a variety of ways. Several years ago I had the opportunity to apply for a position as assistant professor at a large local university. I was a bit nervous about the eight-hour interviewing process, but a few nights before I was to interview my husband had a dream that I was walking around on campus. He felt strongly that God was saying I had the job. Within a few days of the interview, I had been offered the position. There are a multitude of ways the Spirit can speak through others. Oftentimes it is confirmation of what you already know.

God speaks through unanswered prayer

When God is answering our prayers and life seems grand, we feel all is well. However, when we are praying and seeking God and He is silent, we need to relax and let God unfold His perfect plan. Most of us hate waiting on God and His divine timetable. Sometimes "no" or "wait" is His divine sovereignty in your life. If we could learn to relax during these seasons of waiting, our spiritual roots would go deeper as we love and worship Him. "Be still, and know that I am God" (Ps. 46:10) gives us opportunity to quiet our spirits and listen and wait on Him.

Disappointments

Many times when life is not going our way, we become despondent and depressed with the disappointments of life. But when things don't work out like we had hoped, it can be the hand of God intervening in our lives. My first marriage is an example of being devastated by life circumstances. I married my childhood sweetheart, the love of my life, only for the relationship to end in divorce. God hates divorce, but He also gives us free will. When my husband left, I was devastated and overcome with grief and despair. But shortly after the divorce the Lord started opening huge doors of opportunity for me. I was accepted at Peabody College of Vanderbilt University within five months of the divorce to work on a doctorate. I had just completed a master's degree in psychology and made approximately $12,000 a year as a school counselor in the public school system. Finishing my degree and becoming licensed as a psychologist was part of God's plan for my life. Without the divorce, I would have never had the opportunity to accomplish that dream.

I later fell in love with a funny, charismatic guy who broke my heart. He had the audacity to move out of town and never say good-bye. Working through that disappointment brought me so much discontent and restlessness that I quit my job in a community mental health center and went into full-time private practice, which was really scary at the time. I also moved from my hometown in a small, rural community to a city nearby and started life over. This move was one of the best decisions I have made in my life. My daughter and I stepped into a whole new life with boundless opportunities and wonderful new relationships. We started attending a church that allowed us to learn about the Holy Spirit.

We need to learn to fellowship with the Spirit in all circumstances—the good and the disappointing. Accidents don't happen in the kingdom of God. God allows some things and sends others. Tragedy, financial loss, sickness, and affliction are other ways God gets our attention and speaks to us.

Learning to be Sensitive to His Voice

There are many scriptures in the Book of John that make reference to the Spirit leading, guiding, teaching, and speaking to us. John 10:1–4 tells us, "I tell you the truth, the man who does not enter the sheep pen by the gate, but climbs in by some other way, is a thief and a robber. The man who enters by the gate is the shepherd of his sheep. The watchman opens the gate for him, and the sheep listen to his voice. He calls his own sheep by name and leads them out. When he has brought out all his own, he goes on ahead of them, and his sheep follow him because they know his voice." In John 10:27 the Word says, "My sheep listen to my voice; I know them, and they follow me." Many say we are not able to hear the voice of the Spirit, but Scripture clearly states we are expected to hear the voice of the Good Shepherd. How does the Spirit lead us into all truth and guide us if we have no capacity to hear His voice?

Many years ago when I was first saved and baptized in the Holy Spirit, I made a decision I would err on the side of being presumptuous with my "hearing God," as opposed to never trying to learn how to discern His voice and His ways concerning my life. I am the first to say I have missed the mark many times, but it hasn't been because I was not going to Him seeking, asking, and trying to hear. I would rather miss the mark and try to discern and hear the voice of the Spirit, than err in not making any effort at all.

The Lord loves you and desires to communicate with you and tell you great and marvelous things. Your responsibility is to make yourself available to Him. As you are trying to learn to discern His voice, make sure you live in the Word and grow in your knowledge of Scripture. God never tells us anything that does not line up with Scripture.

If you are interested in learning how to interpret dreams, visions, signs, and wonders, then read Chuck Pierce's *When God Speaks*. This book explains the supernatural realm of hearing the Lord and how to be led in His ways.[45]

THINK ABOUT IT

1. Have you had experiences of restlessness? As you reflect on those instances, in hindsight, can you imagine what God may have been telling you?
2. Have you ever had the experience of having someone else confirm a word from God? How did you act on it?
3. Look back on setbacks or disappointments you may have experienced. How did they change your life?

CHAPTER 8

INTERCESSION DIRECTED BY THE HOLY SPIRIT

PRAYING IN THE Holy Spirit gives us the ability to be obedient to the following scripture: "Pray at all times (on every occasion, in every season) in the Spirit, with all [manner of] prayer and entreaty. To that end keep alert and watch with strong purpose and perseverance, interceding in behalf of all the saints (God's consecrated people)" (Eph. 6:18, AMP). I have personally found it to be impossible to pray with my mind and understanding *at all times and without ceasing*. But when you have prayed all you know to pray and you have no other words, you can shift to praying in the Spirit and pray for hours. The Spirit takes us into effortless prayer; however, to be sustained in prayer for long periods of time is hard work. After long periods of focused intercession, you may be tired and feel you have done a day's work. Several years ago I experienced what God spoke to Isaiah when He said His people had not wearied themselves for His sake. In Isaiah 43:18–19 God says, "Forget the former things; do not dwell on the past. See, I am doing a new thing!...Do you not perceive it? I am making a way in the desert." Then He goes on to say, "Yet you have not called upon me, O Jacob, you have not wearied yourselves for me, O Israel. You have not...honored me with your sacrifices" (Isa. 43:22–23).

THE FIRST TIME I WEARIED MYSELF FOR THE LORD

I went to Budapest, Hungary, in 1998 for a Christian–Jewish outreach sponsored by Jonathan Bernis, the president of Jewish Voice Ministries International. Budapest has a large population of Jewish people and many Holocaust survivors. The focus of the week was to have a Jewish festival for three days and invite people from all over the city. I signed up for this event as an intercessor who was to pray for all aspects of the week. Thirty intercessors from all over the world also joined in the concert of prayer offered on behalf of these marvelous people. Our assignment was to pray for three-hour shifts twice a day. My shift was from noon until 3:00 p.m. and from midnight until 3:00 in the morning. I had never prayed for six hours a day by myself, so from the start I was challenged. All of the intercessors gathered together from 9:00 a.m. until noon for prayer, and then my assignment was from noon until 3:00 p.m., so all of us had nine hours a day of focused intercession. Toward the end of the week prior to the actual festival, we were praying sixteen hours a day. Friday, the day the festival started, I prayed for sixteen hours, and during this time went back to my room and fell into my small bed exhausted from the long hours of prayer and aggressive warfare intercession. As I was drifting off to sleep, the Lord spoke and said, "This is what it means to weary yourself on My behalf." I will never forget that day. That ten days in Budapest was a major turning point in my life. I shifted from someone who prayed faithfully for my family and things of personal concern to someone who aggressively warred in the spirit realm over cities and nations. Wearying myself for the Lord in Budapest launched me into a new level of warfare prayer.

Intercession directed by the Holy Spirit guides us into powerful, effective prayer. When prayer connects with the Holy Spirit through praying in the Spirit, you hook up with the divine power source. Much of the time we do not know how to pray as we should, but the Holy Spirit helps us in our weakness. Romans 8:26 says, "In the same way the Spirit also helps our weakness; for we do not know how to pray as we should, but the Spirit Himself intercedes for us with groanings too deep for words" (NASB).

The Holy Spirit prompts us to pray strategic prayers to counter demonic forces and attacks. As you pray in the Spirit, you are praying perfect prayers. Perfect praise and worship destroys the work of the enemy and allows you to grow in faith.

As you begin praying and moving in the gifts of the Spirit, you will start to encounter the spirit of intercession. When you start to move from prayer into intercession, you notice that prayer starts to shift and become more intensive and specific and sometimes more aggressive. Prayer starts to take on a different atmosphere, and you sense you are moving into a higher or different realm. If you are praying in a group, the group will also notice the shift and realize they have shifted into a higher realm of prayer under the direction of the Holy Spirit. I have already mentioned that there is no reference to the spirit of intercession in Scripture, but experientially it is a reality. The Spirit launches your prayers into a higher dimension and realm of the Spirit. At this level of intercession, the Spirit can move forth aggressively. You will sense you have stepped across the battle lines and moved into battle. At this level of intercession, you start to experience various gifts of the Spirit as you pray. You may feel the gifts of faith and prophecy have been released. Or you may start discerning spirits. Visions may occur, and prophetic intercession starts to manifest while interceding.

Intercession directed by the Holy Spirit will often launch you into warfare intercession. At this level you will start to war in the Spirit. The prayer language and gift of tongues are activated for battle. For me personally, when I launch into aggressive warfare intercession, my prayer language is usually different from my usual prayer language. It is easy to discern and know the language is a completely different language. You will start taking authority over the powers of darkness, binding and rebuking the enemy, and breaking generational curses. Your prayer language becomes a weapon of warfare as you move in faith into deeper and higher levels of warring intercession. Breakthroughs come forth after warring in the Spirit.

A word of caution about warfare intercession: Most Christians grow and mature in prayer and find themselves moving into the deeper things of the Spirit when desire and passion are present. You have the authority to fight the enemy over your own life and your family and your sphere of influence. You do not have the spiritual authority to fight powers and principalities of darkness over cities and regions and nations until the Spirit has trained you to go into these particular battles.

I have found the Lord will only let me and prayer groups that I lead or participate in go into these aggressive places in intercession when spiritually strong, like-minded Christians are present. This is for our protection. When certain participants show up for prayer (people who, for whatever reason, are less strong), the Spirit limits where He takes us in prayer. But when we have seven or more strong intercessors who are accustomed to warring in the Spirit, thc Lord will often take us to heights and depths of intercession to which we have never been.

For prayer to be effective, you must learn to be still and sensitive to the moving of the Holy Spirit. It is only by the Spirit that you know how to proceed in prayer, by making declarations or decreeing something to come forth or be released. Only by the Holy Spirit can you discern attacks against you and know how to fight the enemy. We need to learn how to discern the voice of the Lord and the moving of the Spirit so we will understand, overcome, and break through in every situation. God empowers us to pray and prophesy and bind things that must be bound on Earth. He desires for us to bind the things on Earth that need to be bound. In order to know what to bind, we need to have ears to hear. Matthew 11:15 says, "He who has ears to hear, let him hear" (NKJV). Pray that God will open your ears to hear His voice and give you the obedience to obey. Release your faith and trust the Spirit to take you into new realms of glory.

How the Holy Spirit Helps Us in Prayer

In Romans 8:14, Paul discusses our need for the Holy Spirit to guide and lead us in our Christian experience: "For all who are being led by the Spirit of God, these are the sons of God" (NASB). After we have become a Christian, we must be continually led by the Spirit to mature. As we're told in Romans 8:26–27, "So too the [Holy] Spirit comes to our aid and bears us up in our weakness; for we do not know what prayer to offer nor how to offer it worthily as we ought, but the Spirit Himself goes to meet our supplication and pleads in our behalf with unspeakable yearnings and groanings too deep for utterance. And He Who searches the hearts of men knows what is in the mind of the [Holy] Spirit [what His intent is], because the Spirit intercedes and pleads [before God] in behalf of the saints according to and in harmony with God's will" (AMP). Paul is saying we don't know how to pray, nor do we have the strength to pray as we ought. As we allow the Holy Spirit to lead and guide us in prayer, our prayer life will become strong and effective.

In his book *The Holy Spirit in You*, Derek Prince tells us, "The key to effective praying is learning how to be so related to the Holy Spirit that we can submit to Him. Then we can let Him guide, direct, inspire, and strengthen, and many times actually pray through us."[46] One way the Holy Spirit helps us pray is through deep and unspeakable thoughts that cannot be expressed in words. Intercession is often referred to as travail, which means mental or physical work, and also can refer to the labor of childbirth. Prince further states, "No real spiritual reproduction in the church can occur without spiritual travail in prayer. It is when Zion travails that she brings forth sons."[47] He is referring to Isaiah 66:8, which says, "As soon as Zion travailed, she also brought forth her sons" (NASB). Paul further describes intercessory prayer as being the pains of childbirth (see Gal. 4:18–20) or groanings too deep for words, as above.

Paul's powerful prayer written in Colossians 1:9–10 says, "For this reason we also, from the day we heard of it, have not ceased to pray and make [special] request for you, [asking] that you may be filled with the full (deep and clear) knowledge of His will in all spiritual wisdom [in comprehensive insight into the ways and purposes of God] and in understanding and discernment of spiritual things—That you may walk (live and conduct yourselves) in a manner worthy of the Lord, fully pleasing to Him and desiring to please Him in all things, bearing fruit in every good work and steadily growing and increasing in and by the knowledge of God [with fuller, deeper, and clearer insight, acquaintance, and recognition]" (AMP). As we grow and mature in the ways of God, we have access to knowledge of His will in all spiritual wisdom and can discern matters of the Spirit more clearly. As we pray in the Spirit, we have access to the mind of Christ and to spiritual wisdom and insight for prayer that goes beyond our human capacity to know how or what to pray.

WAYS THE HOLY SPIRIT DIRECTS PRAYER

When we tap into the Holy Spirit during our prayer life, He begins to direct us in a variety of ways. The Spirit brings to our minds scripture to pray, words that unfold in prayer, prophetic intercession, a new unknown tongue, visions, and movements in the Spirit that direct and unfold prayer. The Holy Spirit begins to put words into our mouths. Sometimes there can be manifestations of the Spirit that can also confirm and direct intercession. He shows us in our minds what we need to pray and what direction He wants to go to fulfill His prayer assignment.

Words and scripture dropped into your spirit

One way the Spirit directs prayer is by dropping a word into your spirit while you are praying in the Spirit. Developing spiritual ears to hear the voice of the Spirit takes time. You will be amazed how quickly the Lord can teach you to hear His voice through His Spirit. For instance, while you are praying you may hear in your spirit the words *whirlwind of God*. These are not words you would automatically be hearing while praying with your mind (your native language).

The following example may help describe hearing in the Spirit and receiving words in your spirit. You might, in faith, pray something like the following: "I am hearing the words *whirlwind of God*. I am not sure what this means, but I am seeing tornados touching down all over the South." If you had just been praying about revival and all of a sudden you heard "whirlwind of God" and started seeing in your mind's eye (seeing in the Spirit) tornados popping up all over the South, then the Spirit might have been giving you direction while you prayed. If you are seeing tornadoes across the South, you are probably also seeing a map of some sort that would give you specific information about the section of the country for which you are praying. It would be reasonable to think that you are seeing spiritual tornadoes (the whirlwind of God) coming upon the South, bringing great revival in various areas. As you sense these things in the Spirit, you should start to pray accordingly. You may start to pray for revival over the region you are seeing on the map. If you are praying in a prayer group, others in the group will probably start to hear a specific scripture that connects with what the group is hearing and seeing and sensing.

As you follow the lead of the Holy Spirit, you will be *led* in prayer. When the Holy Spirit has been invited to a time of prayer (personal or group), He likes to take over when the participants are yielded to His lead. Prayer becomes exciting when you are praying with your mind and understanding and switch and start praying in the Holy Spirit. The more you pray in the Holy Spirit (tongues), the more you will start seeing and hearing in the Spirit. Prayer will take the direction of the Holy Spirit if you let Him lead. The authority of heaven ignites your prayers. Prayer is much more powerful and hits the target quicker when we move under the power and unction of the Holy Spirit during prayer. The power of the baptism of the Holy Spirit releases you into deeper realms of intercession.

Prophetic intercession

As we spend time with the Lord in prayer, we develop history with Him that opens us up to the gifts of the Spirit, one of which is prophecy. *Webster's Dictionary* describes *prophecy* as "the inspired declaration of divine will and purpose."[48] The Scripture says the Holy Spirit is not only the Spirit of truth (John 6:13), but also the Spirit of prophecy, as stated in Revelation 19:10: "For the substance (essence) of the truth revealed by Jesus is the spirit of all prophecy [the vital breath, the inspiration of all inspired preaching and interpretation of the divine will and purpose, including both mine and yours]" (AMP).

While praying, the Spirit of prophecy may come forth through an intercessor and speak something that God has quickened (stirred up) in that person's spirit. Sometimes you will feel the Spirit of prophecy enter the room; the spiritual atmosphere in the room shifts. Just as we have discussed, the Bible doesn't mention the spirit of intercession, nor the spirit of prophecy; but experientially you become accustomed to the Spirit manifesting in certain ways, such as intercession, prophecy, and so on.

As you sit quietly, you will soon hear someone come forth with a word from the Lord. The person speaking or giving the word speaks of things that are not currently real as though they were. Romans 4:17 depicts someone who can prophesy in the Spirit as one "who gives life to the dead and speaks of the nonexistent things that [He has foretold and promised] as if they [already] existed" (AMP). In prophetic intercession, you call forth the word of the Lord and declare the word and bring it into existence through faith.

In developing the gift of prophecy, you have to develop spiritual ears to hear. Oftentimes we don't hear or discern the word of the Lord due to lack of spiritual maturity and hunger for God. Jesus describes such people in Matthew 13:14, saying, "You will be ever hearing but never understanding; you will be ever seeing but never perceiving." As you grow spiritually, you will begin to discern the voice of your spirit and the voice of the Spirit. In order to develop the discerning ear, you must spend time with the Lord. As you start to cultivate hearing His voice, you will become more confident in speaking forth what you are hearing. Your faith grows as you move in the things of the Spirit, and you will prophesy according to your measure of faith. Praying in groups or corporately will help develop your prophetic gifting, as it stirs your spirit, which in turn will ignite the prophetic gift. One of the incredible benefits of praying in a group is you can learn so much about intercession from each other. The Lord longs to teach His people to pray and to equip them with the power of His Spirit to pray effectively and powerfully. As you develop spiritual ears to hear the Lord and exercise the faith He has given you, you will be amazed how quickly you will start to move in the things of the Spirit.

New, unknown tongue

When you are baptized in the Holy Spirit, you usually have one consistent prayer language. However, as you grow in intercession directed by the Holy Spirit, you may be given a different language or unknown tongue to war in the Spirit over a certain situation. Oftentimes I start my prayer time with thanksgiving and praise and then worship and pray in the Spirit and pray with my mind and understanding. Most days I will ask the Lord to give me the spirit of intercession to help unction (enable) me to pray. As I start moving into intercession, my prayer language (tongue) may change to a totally different language. Usually for me, it becomes aggressive intercession with a warlike tone and shouts and other manifestations of the Spirit. (This will be explained more fully below.) Sometimes the Spirit will reveal to me what I am praying about; other times I simply move and act in faith.

Visions—seeing in the spirit

As you pray, you will start to see things in the spirit. Images will pop up in your mind. Or it may be like a motion picture. One of the most powerful prayer groups I have ever had the opportunity to experience met a couple of years ago. A seasoned intercessor started seeing the Great Wall of China as soon as we started to pray and started forcefully to pray what she was seeing. She carried the meeting (prayed by herself because she had "the prayer") for about twenty minutes, focused in aggressive prayer over China. Her prayer language sounded like Chinese, which was not her regular prayer language. When the Spirit lifted and the prayer for China was finished, she said, "Oh my, I have never prayed for China before. I wonder what all of that was about." She prayed aggressively in the Holy Spirit (tongues) for a while, and then she would shift and pray with understanding (in English); it was as if she were praying the interpretation of what she had prayed in tongues. This is a normal occurrence when praying in the Spirit. While praying in tongues you will often sense you have received the interpretation of what has been prayed.

Other examples of visions would be if you or the group are praying and all of a sudden someone sees fighting going on in some specific city in Iraq. (The pictures are sometimes like a picture from a camera or a scene from a movie: you look—and behold, there is a picture. The same is true for seeing things in the spirit. You simply see a picture of something in your mind's eye.) The group starts praying whatever they are seeing until the Spirit gives complete insight or direction in how to pray, until the prayer seems to be finished in this area and moves to another focus. Recently, my group started seeing children and teenagers by the millions all over the country and knew that we were to move into prayer over the children of the nation and everything that concerns our children. These are just a few examples of how the Holy Spirit moves and shifts prayer by seeing in the Spirit.

Putting words into our mouths

Sometimes when we are praying, words that defy logic and don't seem to make any sense pop out of our mouths. For example, someone in the group may be going through a difficult time and someone is praying over her, when all of a sudden the person praying speaks something specific about a situation she knows nothing about—and yet the prayer hits the mark. After the prayer time, this person may have no idea why she prayed what she did and may have no insight into what she was praying. Sometimes prophetic intercession operates in this way. We speak and prophesy and declare things from the Spirit of which we have no understanding. Words coming forth "out of nowhere" are often prophetic words given by the Holy Spirit. As you grow in intercession, you will be able to discern what gifts are in operation.

Manifestations in the Spirit

This is an interesting topic due to the many unusual manifestations that can come from the Spirit. Some of these manifestations can be offensive to onlookers due to our lack of understanding of spiritual matters. God confounds the wise with things in the spirit that seem to be foolish.

A few years ago, a group of women from a local Nashville church went to the Pensacola Revival. A friend of mine came back from Pensacola with a strange manifestation of the Spirit. She was an intercessor, and every time she came into the sanctuary and worship started, her right arm would start moving in a pounding motion. It looked like she was breaking ground with her arm. The more she moved into intercession and worship, the greater the pounding motion became. During those early days of witnessing manifestations of the Spirit, I was mesmerized by this phenomenon. I would sit close to her or behind her so I could watch this most interesting activity that she apparently had no control over. (She could have refused to yield to the Spirit and stopped the motion; however, since she was yielded to the Holy Spirit, she moved with the Spirit until the motion "lifted.") Finally, one day I asked the Lord, "What on Earth is this about? And why don't I have any manifestation in the Spirit?" The Lord promptly told me that since this woman had yielded to Him in a deep place of obedience while in Pensacola, He had blessed her with a strong intercessory movement that was indicative of breaking ground in the Spirit. He also told me I had no manifestation of His Spirit because, first of all, I didn't realize there was such a thing; secondly, I had never asked; and thirdly, I cared too much what others might think about it because it was a bit unusual. So I said, "OK, Lord, I yield to You and ask for a manifestation of Your Spirit. I don't care what others think about it."

As long as we care more what others think than what God thinks, we stay earthbound in the things of the Spirit. We really have to be more concerned about offending God than we are about offending others. When we come to a place where we don't care how foolish we look if God is glorified, then the Lord has us in a humble place where His Spirit can move through us as a vessel.

Shortly after praying this prayer, I started to notice that when I felt the Spirit strongly, I would shout. This shout could never be predicted, and I had and have no control over it. I started noticing that when I prayed with a friend of mine (usually in a group), I would shout, and then she would shout almost simultaneously. The synchronization between us was so powerful, we had to be on guard in restaurants or other places where we didn't need to be letting out a shout.

Over the years as I have embraced this manifestation, the Lord has intensified it. When I am in a corporate meeting and my spirit strongly bears witness with something spoken or something the Spirit does in the meeting, I will shout. It was given to me to show me when I am on point with something of the Spirit, or when I am praying in agreement with the Spirit, or having thoughts given to me by the Spirit. It has so developed that now when I am praying or alone with the Lord and He is speaking or I am thinking (remember, we have the mind of Christ), I will shout when the Holy Spirit "lands on" something. When the Holy Spirit lands on something, it means you receive a strong witness in your spirit. A witness of the Spirit is developed as you spend time with the Lord. Sometimes it can feel like Holy Spirit goose bumps. Or it may feel like heat that covers you from head to foot, like a massive hot flash. Or the witness of the Spirit may feel like a flood of peace that overwhelms you. It is a deep, inner knowing that you have connected with God in a powerful way.

Sometimes when I feel the presence of the Lord strongly, I can shout a lot during intercession, especially during group intercession. Remember the Spirit stirs the gifts within and among the prayer group, and there may be a flood of manifestations of the Spirit with prophecy, tongues and interpretation, visions, and seeing and hearing the voice of the Spirit. I have so yielded to this strong manifestation of the Spirit that when I see something on television and God is trying to get me to take special note, I will shout while doing dishes, eating, cooking, or whatever I might be doing. My husband has gotten so used to it that he sometimes shouts back, just because it is such a strange phenomenon. He thinks it is funny. And sometimes it is funny! Even my grandchildren are getting accustomed to me doing this. I just say, "Hey, guys. [They are little boys.] Muzzie just had an encounter with the Lord."

There are many other manifestations of the Spirit. One of the intercessors who faithfully prays with us evidently has angelic encounters. We all pace and walk and stand and shout, and Grace is a burden-bearing intercessor. A burden-bearer cries over the things that are on the heart of God. Burden-bearers have sensitive hearts themselves; they feel the burden of the Lord, and weep over whatever the Spirit is bringing up. Grace cries at almost every prayer meeting. I lead the group, but I may not always know what the *heart* of God is for the prayer meeting. I may know His direction and "agenda" in a practical sense, but not His heart. We move into thanksgiving and praise and pray in the Spirit until we sense God's direction. Many times Grace will pick up the burden of the Lord in the Spirit and start to weep. I will then say after a period of time, "Grace, what burden has the Lord given you?" She shares the burden, and then we move from there. Thus, one of the manifestations of the Spirit is burden-bearing. At other times, she may be walking and declaring and prophesying, and it is as if angels are in the room spinning her around. Sometimes she may fall under the power of the Spirit. On these days the room is thick with the presence of the Lord.

Others members of the group may be slain in the Spirit. Being slain in the Spirit means you are usually on the floor because the power of God is so strong on you that you can't get up or move. Sometimes you feel plastered to the floor or in a chair and can't move. Of course, most of the time you *can* move, but sometimes you are so deep into the spirit realm that you can't. During these strong manifestations of His presence, deep, inner healing or spiritual work is being done in our spirits and souls. Sometimes there may be a strong fragrance that may be released in the room. A few months ago when the prayer time was particularly strong, I smelled a strong fragrance of gardenias and cinnamon. I kept looking around the room to see if I could detect who had on the new perfume. After the meeting I asked about the fragrance, and no one had on a new perfume, nor did they smell the fragrance. The intoxicating fragrance was released as God let a bit of heaven touch Earth. Sometimes there can be a strong smell of freshly baked bread. Jesus is sometimes called the Bread of Life, so He may appear as the bread of life in a meeting. This has not happened to me, but I have read about it happening to others. The list of spiritual manifestations is endless. God gives different gifts to each of us. It may not be a spiritual gift as listed in the Scriptures, but it is a gift nonetheless.

✠

The more we ask and the more we exercise our faith to receive the goodness and gifts of God, the more He is willing to pour out His Spirit on all flesh. We're told:

> In the last days, God says, I will pour out my Spirit on all people. Your sons and daughters will prophesy, your young men will see visions, your old men will dream dreams. Even on my servants, both men and women, I will pour out my Spirit in those days, and they will prophesy.
>
> —Acts 2:17–18

This scripture is a reference from Joel 2:28–29. It is a message prophesied hundreds of years before Peter stood and reported what the Hoy Spirit had just poured out in the upper room onto 120 recipients.

Think About It

1. Have you ever received a gift from the Holy Spirit? Did you understand what gift was operating?
2. When does this particular gift operate in your life? Have you been able to embrace it and allow the Holy Spirit to develop it further?
3. Do you have ears to hear and discern the voice of the Spirit? Are you willing to let the Lord teach you how to listen in a deeper way and move deeper into the realm of the Holy Spirit? What obstacles do you think you will have to overcome?
4. Have you ever experienced the gift of prophecy working in your life, other than in prayer?

5. If you are baptized in the Holy Spirit, have you ever switched prayer languages? If so, under what circumstances did this happen? Did you sense you were moving into more aggressive prayer?
6. Do you ever "see" in the Spirit? What form does it take for you? Do you see a picture or do you see a motion picture? Does this occur more in prayer? If not, when?
7. Have you ever felt a word dropping into your mind or out of your mouth and you were a bit shocked or surprised by it?
8. Have you ever experienced a manifestation of the Spirit? How did you feel when you first started experiencing this spiritual phenomenon?

AFTERWORD

As we have seen, the Holy Spirit is an active, creative, powerful person of the Godhead, with God the Father and Jesus the Son. He has been around from the inception of time and is mentioned from Genesis 1:2 until the end of the Book of Revelation. He is the divine power source all through the Old Testament, moving through prophets, kings, and ordinary men and women, establishing and performing His word and unfolding His story—history! He was the power source behind the immaculate conception of Jesus in the Virgin Mary, the power behind Jesus' miracles, and the power that raised Jesus from the dead. He was the power behind Jesus' ascension into heaven and His elevation to be seated at the right hand of God the Father.

The Holy Spirit is the One who draws and woos us to Jesus during our conversion and salvation process. He is the One who baptizes us in His Spirit and gives us gifts to advance His kingdom. He longs for us to love Him, to know Him, and to serve Him. He is waiting for you to yield your life totally to Him so that He can take you into deeper realms of His glory. After your salvation, the baptism in the Holy Spirit is your gateway into the power that will allow you to grow into spiritual maturity.

Our salvation and the empowerment by the Spirit of the living God was never to be about bowing our knee to the opinions of man and living in the fear of what others think. The Holy Spirit has set us free from worthless lives lived in vain, and He offers us the key to salvation and empowerment through hunger and thirst for God.

It is my hope that you will prayerfully read the many Scripture references that follow and ask the Holy Spirit to reveal and teach you truth about Himself. I pray you will be saved, water baptized, and yield your life to the baptism of the Holy Spirit, which is a door of power into the things of the Spirit. Never allow anyone to intimidate you or discourage you from hungering and seeking the truth of God's Word. Allow the Holy Spirit to reveal His truth to you and yield to and invite Him to invade your life. You will never be the same as you move forward on your earthly pilgrimage to your heavenly home.

May the power and glory and dominion of the Holy Spirit rest upon and in you as you press on to walk in His truth and love.

SCRIPTURES RELATED TO THE HOLY SPIRIT

Now the earth was formless and empty, darkness was over the surface of the deep, and the Spirit of God was hovering over the waters.

—Genesis 1:2

Then the Lord said, "My Spirit will not contend with man forever, for he is mortal; his days will be a hundred and twenty years."

—Genesis 6:3

Then the Lord came down in the cloud and spoke with him, and he took of the Spirit that was on him and put the Spirit on the seventy elders. When the Spirit rested on them, they prophesied, but they did not do so again.

—Numbers 11:25

The woman gave birth to a boy and named him Samson. He grew and the Lord blessed him, and the Spirit of the Lord began to stir him while he was in Mahaneh Dan, between Zorah and Eshtaol.

—Judges 13:24–25

When they arrived at Gibeah, a procession of prophets met him; the Spirit of God came upon him in power, and he joined in their prophesying.

—1 Samuel 10:10

So Samuel took the horn of oil and anointed him in the presence of his brothers, and from that day on the

Spirit of the Lord came upon David in power...Now the Spirit of the Lord had departed from Saul, and an evil spirit from the Lord tormented him.

—1 Samuel 16:13–14

You gave your good Spirit to instruct them.

—Nehemiah 9:20

For many years you were patient with them. By your Spirit you admonished them through your prophets.

—Nehemiah 9:30

The Spirit of God has made me; the breath of the Almighty gives me life.

—Job 33:4

Do not cast me from your presence or take your Holy Spirit from me.

—Psalm 51:11

For they rebelled against the Spirit of God, and rash words came from Moses' lips.

—Psalm 106:33

Where can I go from your Spirit? Where can I flee from your presence?

—Psalm 139:7

Teach me to do your will, for you are my God; may your good Spirit lead me on level ground.

—Psalm 143:10

The Spirit of the Lord will rest on him—the Spirit of wisdom and of understanding, the Spirit of counsel and of power, the Spirit of knowledge and of the fear of the LORD—and he will delight in the fear of the LORD.

—ISAIAH 11:2–3

"Woe to the obstinate children," declares the LORD, "to those who carry out plans that are not mine, forming an alliance, but not by my Spirit, heaping sin upon sin.

—ISAIAH 30:1

Till the Spirit is poured upon us from on high, and the desert becomes a fertile field, and the fertile field seems like a forest.

—ISAIAH 32:15

For I will pour water on the thirsty land, and streams on the dry ground; I will pour out my Spirit on your offspring, and my blessing on your descendants.

—ISAIAH 44:3

The Spirit of the Sovereign LORD is on me, because the LORD has anointed me to preach good news to the poor.

—ISAIAH 61:1

Yet they rebelled and grieved his Holy Spirit.

—ISAIAH 63:10

And afterward, I will pour out my Spirit on all people. Your sons and daughters will prophesy, your old men will dream dreams, your young men will see visions. Even on my servants, both men and women, I will pour out my Spirit in those days.

—JOEL 2:28–29

So he said to me, "This is the word of the Lord to Zerubbabel: 'Not by might nor by power, but by my Spirit,' says the Lord Almighty."

—Zechariah 4:6

I baptize you with water for repentance. But after me will come one who is more powerful than I, whose sandals I am not fit to carry. He will baptize you with the Holy Spirit and with fire.

—Matthew 3:11

As soon as Jesus was baptized, he went up out of the water. At that moment heaven was opened, and he saw the Spirit of God descending like a dove and lighting on him.

—Matthew 3:16

Then Jesus was led by the Spirit into the desert to be tempted by the devil.

—Matthew 4:1

At that time you will be given what to say, for it will not be you speaking, but the Spirit of your Father speaking through you.

—Matthew 10:19–20

And so I tell you, every sin and blasphemy will be forgiven men, but the blasphemy against the Spirit will not be forgiven.

—Matthew 12:31

All authority in heaven and on earth has been given to me. Therefore go and make disciples of all nations, baptizing them in the name of the Father and of the Son and of the Holy Spirit, and teaching them to obey everything I have commanded you. And surely I am with you always, to the very end of the age.

—Matthew 28:18–20

I baptize you with water, but he will baptize you with the Holy Spirit.

—Mark 1:8

The angel answered, "The Holy Spirit will come upon you, and the power of the Most High will overshadow you. So the holy one to be born will be called the Son of God."

—Luke 1:35

The Spirit of the Lord is on me, because he has anointed me to preach good news to the poor.

—Luke 4:18

Which of you fathers, if your son asks for a fish, will give him a snake instead? Or if he asks for an egg, will give him a scorpion? If you then, though you are evil, know how to give good gifts to your children, how much more will your Father in heaven give the Holy Spirit to those who ask him!

—Luke 11:11–13

The man on whom you see the Spirit come down and remain is he who will baptize with the Holy Spirit.

—John 1:33

Jesus answered, "I tell you the truth, no one can enter the kingdom of God unless he is born of water and the Spirit. Flesh gives birth to flesh, but the Spirit gives birth to spirit. You should not be surprised at my saying, 'You must be born again.' The wind blows wherever it pleases. You hear its sound, but you cannot tell where it comes from or where it is going. So it is with everyone born of the Spirit."

—JOHN 3:5–8

The Spirit gives life; the flesh counts for nothing. The words I have spoken to you are spirit and they are life. Yet there are some of you who do not believe.

—JOHN 6:63–64

Jesus stood and said in a loud voice, "If anyone is thirsty, let him come to me and drink. Whoever believes in me, as the Scripture has said, streams of living water will flow from within him." By this he meant the Spirit, whom those who believed in him were later to receive. Up to that time the Spirit had not been given, since Jesus had not yet been glorified.

—JOHN 7:37–39

But the Counselor, the Holy Spirit, whom the Father will send in my name, will teach you all things and will remind you of everything I have said to you. Peace I leave with you; my peace I give you. I do not give to you as the world gives. Do not let your hearts be troubled and do not be afraid.

—JOHN 14:26–27

But when he, the Spirit of truth, comes, he will guide you into all truth.

—JOHN 16:13

And with that he breathed on them and said, "Receive the Holy Spirit. If you forgive anyone his sins, they are forgiven; if you do not forgive them, they are not forgiven."

—JOHN 20:22–23

On one occasion, while he was eating with them, he gave them this command: "Do not leave Jerusalem, but wait for the gift my Father promised, which you have heard me speak about. For John baptized with water, but in a few days you will be baptized with the Holy Spirit."

—Acts 1:4–5

But you will receive power when the Holy Spirit comes on you; and you will be my witnesses in Jerusalem, and in all Judea and Samaria, and to the ends of the earth.

—Acts 1:8

All of them were filled with the Holy Spirit and began to speak in other tongues as the Spirit enabled them.

—Acts: 2:4

Peter replied, "Repent and be baptized, every one of you, in the name of Jesus Christ for the forgiveness of your sins. And you will receive the gift of the Holy Spirit."

—Acts 2:38

After they prayed, the place where they were meeting was shaken. And they were all filled with the Holy Spirit and spoke the word of God boldly.

—Acts 4:31

When the apostles in Jerusalem heard that Samaria had accepted the word of God, they sent Peter and John to them. When they arrived, they prayed for them that they might receive the Holy Spirit, because the Holy Spirit had not yet come upon any of them; they had simply been baptized into the name of the Lord Jesus.

Then Peter and John placed their hands on them, and they received the Holy Spirit.

—ACTS 8:14–17

Then Ananias went to the house and entered it. Placing his hands on Saul, he said, "Brother Saul, the Lord—Jesus, who appeared to you on the road as you were coming here—has sent me so that you may see again and be filled with the Holy Spirit."

—ACTS 9:17

While Peter was still speaking these words, the Holy Spirit came on all who heard the message. The circumcised believers who had come with Peter were astonished that the gift of the Holy Spirit had been poured out even on the Gentiles. For they heard them speaking in tongues and praising God.

—ACTS 10:44–46

As I began to speak, the Holy Spirit came on them as he had come on us at the beginning. Then I remembered what the Lord had said: "John baptized with water, but you will be baptized with the Holy Spirit."

—ACTS 11:15–16

While they were worshiping the Lord and fasting, the Holy Spirit said, "Set apart for me Barnabas and Saul for the work to which I have called them."

—ACTS 13:2

While Apollos was at Corinth, Paul took the road through the interior and arrived at Ephesus. There he found some disciples and asked them, "Did you receive the Holy Spirit when you believed?" They answered, "No, we have not even heard that there is a Holy Spirit." So Paul asked, "Then what baptism did you receive?" "John's baptism," they replied. Paul said, "John's baptism was a baptism of repentance. He told the people to believe in the one coming after him, that is, in Jesus." On hearing this, they were baptized into the name of the Lord Jesus. When Paul placed his hands on them, the Holy Spirit came on them, and they spoke in tongues and prophesied.

—Acts 19:1–6

And so he condemned sin in sinful man, in order that the righteous requirements of the law might be fully met in us, who do not live according to the sinful nature but according to the Spirit.

Those who live according to the sinful nature have their minds set on what that nature desires; but those who live in accordance with the Spirit have their minds set on what the Spirit desires. The mind of sinful man is death, but the mind controlled by the Spirit is life and peace.

—Romans 8:3–6

You, however, are controlled not by the sinful nature but by the Spirit, if the Spirit of God lives in you. And if anyone does not have the Spirit of Christ, he does not belong to Christ.

—Romans 8:9

In the same way, the Spirit helps us in our weakness. We do not know what we ought to pray for, but the Spirit himself intercedes for us with groans that words cannot express. And he who searches our hearts knows the mind of the Spirit, because the Spirit intercedes for the saints in accordance with God's will.

—Romans 8:26–27

But God has revealed it to us by his Spirit. The Spirit searches all things, even the deep things of God. For who among men knows the thoughts of a man except the man's spirit within him? In the same way no one knows the thoughts of God except the Spirit of God.

—1 Corinthians 2:10–11

The man without the Spirit does not accept the things that come from the Spirit of God, for they are foolishness to him, and he cannot understand them, because they are spiritually discerned.

—1 Corinthians 2:14

Do you not know that your body is a temple of the Holy Spirit, who is in you, whom you have received from God? You are not your own; you were bought at a price. Therefore honor God with your body.

—1 Corinthians 6:19–20

For we were all baptized by one Spirit into one body—whether Jews or Greeks, slave or free—and we were all given the one Spirit to drink.

—1 Corinthians 12:13

Now the Lord is the Spirit, and where the Spirit of the Lord is, there is freedom.

—2 Corinthians 3:17

Now it is God who has made us for this very purpose and has given us the Spirit as a deposit, guaranteeing what is to come.

—2 Corinthians 5:5

So I say, live by the Spirit, and you will not gratify the desires of the sinful nature. For the sinful nature desires what is contrary to the Spirit, and the Spirit what is contrary to the sinful nature. They are in conflict with each other, so that you do not do what you want. But if you are led by the Spirit, you are not under law.

—Galatians 5:16–18

But the fruit of the Spirit is love, joy, peace, patience, kindness, goodness, faithfulness, gentleness and self-control. Against such things there is no law.

—Galatians 5:22–23

The one who sows to please his sinful nature, from that nature will reap destruction; the one who sows to please the Spirit, from the Spirit will reap eternal life. Let us not become weary in doing good, for at the proper time we will reap a harvest if we do not give up.

—Galatians 6:8–9

There is one body and one Spirit—just as you were called to one hope when you were called—one Lord, one faith, one baptism; one God and Father of all, who is over all and through all and in all.

—Ephesians 4:4–6

And do not grieve the Holy Spirit of God, with whom you were sealed for the day of redemption. Get rid of all bitterness, rage and anger, brawling and slander, along with every form of malice. Be kind and compassionate to one another, forgiving each other, just as in Christ God forgave you.

—Ephesians 4:30–32

Take the helmet of salvation and the sword of the Spirit, which is the word of God. And pray in the Spirit on all occasions with all kinds of prayers and requests.

—Ephesians 6:17–18

For prophecy never had its origin in the will of man, but men spoke from God as they were carried along by the Holy Spirit.

—2 Peter 1:21

But you, dear friends, build yourselves up in your most holy faith and pray in the Holy Spirit. Keep yourselves in God's love as you wait for the mercy of our Lord Jesus Christ to bring you to eternal life.

—Jude 20–21

He who has an ear, let him hear what the Spirit says to the churches. To him who overcomes, I will give the right to eat from the tree of life, which is in the paradise of God.

—Revelation 2:7

NOTES

1. Derek Prince, *The Holy Spirit in You* (New Kensington, PA: Whitaker House, 1987).
2. Ibid.
3. Billy Graham, *The Holy Spirit: Activating God's Power in Your Life* (Nashville, TN: W Publishing Group, 1987).
4. Benny Hinn, *Good Morning, Holy Spirit* (Nashville, TN: Thomas Nelson, Inc., 1990).
5. John Sherrill, *They Speak with Other Tongues* (Old Tappan, NJ: Pyramid Publications, 1964), 107–108.
6. Hinn, *Good Morning Holy Spirit*, 10–11.
7. Prince, *The Holy Spirit in You*, 33.
8. Ibid.
9. Dave Roberson, *The Walk of the Spirit—The Walk of Power: The Vital Role of Praying in Tongues* (Tulsa, OK: Dave Roberson Ministries, 1999).
10. Ibid., 395.
11. Ibid.
12. Ibid., 397–398.
13. Ibid., 398.
14. Ibid., 167.
15. Brenda C. Rambo, *Prayer Activation: Level I—Basic Prayer* (Nashville, TN: BRI Publishing, 2008).
16. James Goll, *The Lost Art of Intercession: Restoring the Power and Passion of the Watch of the Lord* (Shippensburg, PA: Destiny Image Publishers, Inc., 1997).
17. Ibid.
18. Ibid., 18.
19. Ibid., 18–19.
20. Ibid., 40.
21. Dennis and Rita Bennett, *The Holy Spirit and You* (Plainfield, NJ: Logos International, 1971), 78.
22. Ibid.

23. Ibid., 79.
24. Ibid., 82.
25. Rodney M. Howard-Browne, *Flowing in the Holy Ghost* (Louisville, KY: RHBEA Publications, 1991), 11.
26. Dave Buehring, *A Discipleship Journey: A Navigational Guide to Spiritual Formation and Mentoring* (Franklin, TN: Ocean Hill Communications, 2004), 229–232.
27. Howard-Browne, *Flowing in the Holy Ghost.*
28. Bennett and Bennett, *The Holy Spirit and You.*
29. Ibid., 140.
30. Buehring, *Discipleship Journey*, 229.
31. Bennett and Bennett, *The Holy Spirit and You*, 155.
32. Ibid., 159.
33. Howard-Browne, *Flowing in the Holy Ghost*, 101.
34. Ibid., 103.
35. Ibid., 107.
36. Ibid.
37. Bennett and Bennett, *The Holy Spirit and You*, 149.
38. Howard-Browne, *Flowing in the Holy Ghost*, 49.
39. Bennett and Bennett, *The Holy Spirit and You*, 114.
40. Howard-Browne, *Flowing in the Holy Ghost*, 68.
41. Bennett and Bennett, *The Holy Spirit and You,* 40.
42. Ibid., 84.
43. Howard-Brown, *Flowing in the Holy Ghost*, 39.
44. Charles Stanley, *How to Listen to God* (Nashville, TN: Oliver-Nelson Books, 1985).
45. Chuck Pierce and Rebecca Wagner Sytsema, *When God Speaks* (Ventura, CA: Regal, 2005).
46. Prince, *The Holy Spirit in You*, 69.
47. Ibid., 71.
48. *Merriam-Webster Online Dictionary*, www.m-w.com, s.v. "prophecy," accessed March 9, 2010.

ABOUT THE AUTHOR

Dr. Brenda Rambo received her doctorate in human development counseling from Peabody College of Vanderbilt University and is a licensed psychologist/health service provider. She is the president of Rambo & Associates, PLLC, a successful private practice working with men and women, children and teenagers, couples and families. She has been a full-time assistant graduate professor at a large southern university, a workshop and retreat speaker, and has lectured nationally and internationally.

As an intercessor, Dr. Rambo focuses on praying for the government, calling intercessors to stand and fight for our nation and to return to our godly heritage. She teaches on such subjects as basic prayer, intercession directed by the Holy Spirit, and how to contend for the blessings and promises of God. Dr. Rambo believes that experiencing the power of the Holy Spirit opens the door to spiritual, emotional, and physical transformation, one life at a time. She currently resides in Nashville with her husband, Mike. They have two children and five grandchildren.

Dr. Rambo is also the founder and president of Life Transformations, Inc., which focuses on extending hope to the hopeless and proclaims that God is the One who "restores the soul" (Ps. 23:3). Life Transformations is dedicated to teaching people how to be God-seekers, establishing a solid spiritual foundation on which they can build productive, meaningful lives and discover their purpose for living.

Empowering women to walk in confidence, find their unique voice, and achieve their highest goals, Life Transformations for

Women helps women develop internal resources, talents, and abilities with God as their source. Practical life application of God's Word in the midst of daily challenges encourages women to rise up and go beyond merely surviving to conquering and overcoming. Life Transformations also provides financial assistance to mothers and children in need.

To Contact the Author

drbrendarambo@comcast.net